Frugal Cool:
How to Get Rich–
Without Making Very Much Money

John F. Gaski, Ph.D.

Foreword by Ara Parseghian

D1065938

Corby Books
Notre Dame, Indiana

Frugal Cool: How to Get Rich–
Without Making Very Much Money

Copyright © 2009 John F. Gaski, Ph.D.

10 9 8 7 6 5 4 3

ISBN 978-0-9776458-6-2

Manufactured in the United States of America

Published by Corby Books
A Division of Corby Publishing
P.O. Box 93
Notre Dame, Indiana 46556
(574) 784-3482
www.corbypublishig.com

To my beloved mother and father,
the best parents a son could have

Acknowledgments

I am indebted to the peerless Ara Parseghian for the Foreword to
this book, to cartoonist Mike Wallace for providing
the illustration, and to Juanita Dix and the folks at Corby Books
for their expert work on production of our finished product.

Table of Contents

Foreword by Ara Parseghian x

Chapter 1   START THINKING DIFFERENTLY ABOUT MONEY........1

Chapter 2   CASE HISTORIES: YOU, TOO, COULD DO THIS 9

Chapter 3   THE PHILOSOPHY AND PSYCHOLOGY OF MONEY
             OR HAVING THE RIGHT ATTITUDE...............................45
             Asceticism and Deferred Gratification.....................................46
             Dedication, Determination, or Obsession? 51
             Self-Management Techniques 52
                 Environmental Control..52
                 Covert Conditioning 54
                 Self-Reward and Self-Punishment 59
                 Self-Observation 61

Chapter 4   OTHER WAYS TO "PSYCH" YOURSELF INTO
             GETTING IT DONE 69
             True Grit From Real Life 82

Chapter 5   PRACTICAL PRINCIPLES AND TACTICS:
             SOME DETAILS ON HOW TO MAKE IT HAPPEN 95
             Major Tactical Directions...98
                 To Budget or Not to Budget..98
                 Life-Cycle Decisions 99
                 A Basic Principle of Personal Finance............................... 108
                 Manna, or Moolah, from Heaven 111

Chapter 6   BACK TO BASICS: A COMPENDIUM OF MONEY-
             SAVING TIPS (IF YOU'RE READY FOR THIS)......................121

Chapter 7   UNCOMMON ADVICE ON GETTING RICH *FAST* 143
            GRQS #1: Cosmetics, Midgets, and Dare To Be Great 144
            GRQS #2: The $745,000 "Hammer" 146
            GRQS #3: $610,000! I Could Cry 149
            GRQS #4: The Textbook Approach 151
            GRQS #4a: The Textbook 155
            Take a Chance, He Says? 158

Chapter 8   FINALLY, A SURE THING *OR* NOW THAT YOU'RE
            BEGINNING TO GET RICH, WHAT DO YOU DO
            WITH ALL THAT MONEY? 163
            Take What the Boss and the Government Give You 163
            Take What the Markets Give You 166
            The Right Answer 168
                Implication #1 171
                Implication #2 172
                Implication #3 172
                The Ultimate Implication 172
            Related Horror Stories 173
            There's No Place Like Home 179
                I. 179
                II. 181
            Remember, It's Only a Game 182

Chapter 9   RECAPITULATION, REINFORCEMENT, AND
            EXTENSION OF PRINCIPLES: PUTTING IT
            ALL TOGETHER 185
Endnotes 197
About the Author 203

Introduction

Yes, it *can* be done—and this book proves it. Not only that, but *Frugal Cool: How to Get Rich* explicitly *shows* the reader how to gain wealth *even without high income*. The book is a combination step-by-step tutorial, demonstration, motivational pep-talk, and philosophical immersion, blended to produce a result that is no less than a miracle—by conventional standards—for the average reader.

This volume is anything but conventional, though. Beyond teaching the most valuable financial lesson most people could hope to receive, *Frugal Cool: How to Get Rich* also reveals that its unique approach to wealth is amazingly simple. Riches can be achieved easily, without any real effort, and, as promised, without making a lot of money; it is all a matter of attitude. Skeptics need only read on. Best of all, perhaps, the book illustrates how much *fun* it can be to "get rich without making very much money," and provides motivation to do just that.

A Foreword by Ara Parseghian*

When I first became head football coach at the University of Notre Dame in 1964, we faced many challenges and long odds. I inherited a team that had won two and lost seven the previous year. Yet I realized that by applying the methods I knew to be sound, we would have a chance to succeed even from the beginning—which we were fortunate enough to do.

What does this have to do with Professor Gaski's program for financial success? A great deal, it turns out. Teaching people to succeed at achieving an objective, whether in football, personal finance, or life in general, involves the application of common and universal principles. Aside from the technical particulars, that is, the "X's and O's" of blocking and tackling, football is largely a matter of motivation, inspiration, commitment, discipline, and organization. Directing a football team, in other words, is a management process, similar to directing any other operation or—now we get to it—Dr. Gaski's prescribed route to financial success. That route, as you shall see, includes appropriate dosages of *motivation, commitment, organization,* and so forth.

One big difference between the self-management regimen of this book and organizational management such as football coaching is that the Gaski method is *much easier on you.* (He doesn't require you to run wind-sprints, for example!) So receive the motivation that this volume offers, allow yourself to be inspired, apply the minimal necessary amount of organization, and commit yourself to the goal—and then only a reasonable degree of self-discipline should be necessary to adhere to the prescribed program for accomplishing your financial aims.

Just as I knew success on the gridiron was likely to follow from enacting the principles I had incorporated into my coaching methods and strategy, Professor Gaski has grounds to be confident that *your* acceptance and application of his principles will produce success for you. Though we all understand that nothing is foolproof when it comes to trying to influence human behavior, whether the humans are football players or self-help book readers, I encourage you to read on and give the material a chance to benefit you. I hope you take to the book's "coaching" in a way that is productive for you.

———————

*Mr. Parseghian is Chairman of the Ara Parseghian Medical Research Foundation and Ara Parseghian Enterprises. Previously he had a renowned career as a football coach, serving as head coach at Miami (Ohio) University (1951-55), Northwestern University (1956-63), and the University of Notre Dame (1964-74) where his teams won two national championships (1966, '73) and shared a third (1964). Ara Parseghian was elected to the College Football Hall of Fame in 1980.

At his own Hall of Fame enshrinement ceremony in 2008, legendary Penn State coach Joe Paterno said, "There's never been a better college football coach than Ara Parseghian."

Contributions to the Ara Parseghian Medical Research Foundation can be sent to 3530 E. Campo Abierto, Suite 105, Tucson, AZ 85718-3327.

Chapter 1

Start Thinking Differently About Money

It's easy. Really, it's much easier than you think. It is not only possible, it's actually easy for the average person to become wealthy, and you don't even have to make a lot of money to do it. No, that is not a paradox, and I'm going to show you how to accomplish it, that is, get rich without making a lot of money.

Sound implausible? Of course it does. Perhaps you've just never thought about it. Or, more likely, you have been conditioned (brainwashed?) by the conventional view of personal finance to focus on the wrong thing. Conventional thinking on money and wealth focuses on only half of the equation—how to make it. The reason this is the wrong perspective is that getting rich by *making* money is out of reach for most people. However, there is another avenue to wealth and prosperity that *is* attainable by most people, and that is what we will concentrate our attention on here.

To see how easy it is to get rich *without making very much money,* the key idea to understand is the concept of *personal profit.* In business, profit is the difference or spread between revenue and expenses, between sales revenue and costs, between what is taken in and what is paid out. It is no different for the individual as an economic entity. The difference between income (from sources such as wages or salary and investment returns) and spending (for living expenses and other consumption) for a given time period may be thought of as one's *personal profit*. The amount of personal profit accumulated over time is a person's wealth or net worth. Obviously, therefore, the key to attaining personal wealth is not income but the *difference* between income and outflow or spending. Generating income, i.e., making money, is only one way of gaining wealth. The other way of enlarging the "personal profit" spread is by controlling expenditure, and unless you are assured of earning a very high income, this is the more realistic alternative for you.

So that's all there is to it—limiting spending? Doesn't everybody know that? And if it's so easy, why doesn't everyone do it?

There appear to be a number of reasons, largely unnecessary, why everyone does not do it. In other words, there are several needless or irrational impediments to getting rich the easy way. They are:

1. Ignorance—ignorance of the very possibility of doing it. Most people have literally never heard of how getting rich without making a lot of money can be done, and have not thought of it themselves. But then, most great ideas are developed by only a few rather than many and I modestly submit that getting rich easily, without making a lot of money, qualifies as a great idea.

2. Even if the idea has occurred or been presented to someone, it is difficult to accept. People simply can't believe it, so they don't even try it. Of course, this is understandable because of the conditioning problem mentioned earlier. People are locked into the conventional and erroneous perspective that making money is *the* way to get rich, and this stifles their chances. Once more for emphasis, *making large amounts of money is not the best way of becoming wealthy* for most people, because it is unattainable. Fortunately, there is another way, an easy way, that will be described in detail in this book.

3. Finally, the approach to getting wealthy recommended here probably does not seem like much fun to those who haven't tried it. Saving money, because it appears to imply not spending and not *consuming*, is not most people's idea of a good time. Therefore, even if a person is

aware of the possibility or opportunity of getting rich without making much money and has accepted it as achievable, he or she is not likely to attempt such a pursuit because it does not appear desirable. Its "costs" or sacrifices are believed to outweigh the benefits.

All these reactions are unnecessary and financially debilitating, and can easily be proven so and disposed of. The rest of this volume is dedicated to (a) demonstrating the validity of the idea that great wealth can be had without the benefit of a high income, (b) proving the practical possibility of this premise and showing *how* it can be done, and (c) persuading the reader that such a course of action is also enjoyable activity. In other words, we will try to overcome prevailing ignorance or inertia, and knock down the destructive myths, so the reader will be able and willing to get rich the easy way—without having to make a lot of money!

The first myth to be dispelled is the idea that getting rich without making very much money is a paradox. It is not at all. The key distinction to recognize is between amount of money made and amount of money retained, or between income and wealth (again, the notion of personal profit, commonly known as "surplus"). Suppose a relatively low-paid worker such as an unskilled manual laborer or a waitress makes $20,000 per year. It would be universally agreed that this person does not make very much money. But even if this low income remains *constant* over a standard 45-year working career, the person will have earned a total of $900,000 during that time period. If somehow the worker could save 50% of his or her income, living on $10,000 a year (as many people do), total wealth would be $450,000 by the end of the period even without earning any returns from investment of the surplus. Most would agree that is a great deal of money. Obviously, one can have a lot of money without making very much money; little money *earned* can translate into *having* great wealth. Different perspectives apply to money retained over time and money earned.

Of course, a 45-year time horizon is too long for most people to be willing to wait (and I certainly would not impose such a delay in delivering what the title of this book promises). So it should also be noted that after only ten years in the context of the preceding example, retained wealth would be $100,000, again *not even taking into account investment earnings* on the $10,000 annual savings. If you had savings of $100,000 or more, would you consider yourself well-off? I would not, because I've been on the program described in this book for about 30-35 years and save much more than $10,000 a year (though I do not make a lot of money), but most people would. The point is that even a relatively low-paid person can become reasonably wealthy fairly *quickly*, as long as the savings rate is high. It will also be shown that this can be done *easily*. And if a 50% saving rate and living on about $10,000 a year seem unrealistic to you, I will demonstrate otherwise.

Now, for more precision and realism, and to provide a more concrete reference point, I offer the projections in Table 1-1. These report the value of the $10,000 annual savings stream over various time periods from five to 40 years, this time taking into account *investment* of the savings, as would and should occur, at an after-tax rate of return of 8%. That rate is very reasonable and achievable. It is approximately the same as the return on tax-free, long-term municipal bonds in some recent years (at the time this was being written), and is a conservative expression of the after-tax return on the *average* common stock portfolio in recent decades (12% before taxes over the last 25-30 years on average, about 18% during the 1980's and '90's. More on how ridiculously easy it is to make money in the stock market will be presented in a later chapter. Yes, that is still true now, especially now.)

As can be seen in the table, after only five years on such a program—$10,000 a year @ 8%, with income reinvested—the individual earner/saver/investor is well on the way to becoming wealthy with a nest egg of $63,359.

Where were you and what were you doing exactly ten years ago? Think about it. Take the time span between then and now, and extend

TABLE 1-1

SAVINGS AND INVESTMENT PROJECTIONS

Future Value

$10,000 annual savings invested at 8% net over:

5 years	$ 63,359
10 years	$ 156,455
20 years	$ 494,228
40 years	$2,797,802

$5000 annual savings invested at 8% net over:

5 years	$ 31,680
10 years	$ 78,227
20 years	$ 247,114
40 years	$1,398,901

that short time period into the future, and that soon you can have over $156,000! Is that too long to wait? Well, you're probably going to be alive in ten years. Would you prefer the alternative of *not* having $156,000? And how would you like having half a million dollars in twenty years? Could you find a use for that much money? Would that amount of wealth make your retirement more comfortable? Or might you be able to retire *sooner* if you worked toward gaining and retaining that amount of money? Do as I tell you, and all this will be possible, easy, and fun. And, obviously, a person in his or her early 20's who abides by this prescribed regimen over an entire working career (the 40-year future value) inevitably becomes super-rich (by the average person's standards, $2.8 million worth!).

If, like most people, you don't believe yet that you can save anywhere near $10,000 per year, inspect the second set of numbers in Table 1-1, which shows lesser but still very substantial wealth values for the respective time intervals. Personally, I do not believe these amounts are as realistic as the first set because I think most people *can* save $10,000 a year with the right information and motivation, as will be presented throughout the rest of this volume. But just for the sake of illustration, the second group of projections is based on annual saving of $5000. Can you handle that? It's only $416.67 a month or $96.15 a week! Frankly, I think you should be able to do much better than that, much better than $31,680 after five years and $78,227 after ten years, etc., because I know of people who have done better than that on income of little more than about $20,000 a year. (You are going to meet some of those and other interesting people soon.) I, myself, do much better than that and will be giving you the benefit of what I know in the forthcoming pages.

What, if anything, have you learned so far? To this point, a number of things should have been established.

• Personal wealth does not depend on income. High income is not a sufficient condition for great wealth, obviously, if spending is also high. Nor is it a necessary condition or prerequisite if spending is low. Individual wealth is a direct function of the *relationship* between income and spending, i.e., "personal profit."

• Most people have considered only one of the two fundamental approaches to getting rich, high income, completely ignoring the easier, more accessible, route to riches that is the focus of this book.

• Once you recognize the difference between *making* a lot of money and *having* a lot of money, that is, the distinction between income and wealth, it becomes apparent how great wealth can be achieved without the benefit of great income. In the language of accountants, income is a *flow*, wealth is a *stock* (as in quantity or amount). Income is measured over a period of time, wealth is measured at a point in time. Income and wealth are totally different creatures. Comparing the two is like comparing apples and oranges, sort of; the two are evaluated on the basis of completely different standards. So, obviously, low income can translate into high wealth if (a) the time period covered is long enough or (b) the retention or saving rate is high enough. That is the fundamental premise of this argument, and acceptance of it is your key to financial independence, prosperity, and riches.

Finally, considering the approach to financial security advocated here, a couple of things should be noted and understood. First, the only real requirement on your part is a new way of thinking. That should be apparent from the central assertion of the book's title. If you appreciate and understand the points enumerated above about the distinction between wealth and income, and how most people unfortunately are not aware of the implications of this difference as far as their personal situations are concerned, you are well on your way to internalizing the needed perspective that will enable you to get rich without making very much money.

Second, and perhaps best of all, once this new way of thinking has been adopted *you don't even have to do anything!* That's the beauty of it. You don't have to do a darned thing to make yourself rich without making a lot of money! It is all, and only, a matter of what you *don't* do. That is what I meant when I stated that it is not only possible, it is *easy*, to accomplish what this book's title promises. (What could be easier than not having to do anything?) Details of how all this can be arranged will be revealed presently—right after some brief, more personal, messages:

You may be wondering why I bother to take the time to impart information on this topic. I don't wonder about it at all. Ever since I first realized that I know something about personal finance that hardly anyone else seems to understand, I have had a natural philanthropic desire (among other motives) to publicly disseminate the information. (Hey, I'm just that kind of guy, O.K.? Besides, your doing well is no "skin off my nose.") This knowledge, it is clear, has the potential to revolutionize your financial condition *and life*, as it has done mine. Widespread application of the principles I offer also could favorably affect our nation's economy. I believe I might experience real satisfaction from transmitting such benefit and impact—so I do not deny that type of personal motivation.

Be prepared for something very unusual in the opus to follow. This is not your run-of-the-mill personal finance "how-to" book, though it properly fits in the how-to, self-help, personal finance category. It is not a "get rich quick" book. Neither is it a "get rich slowly but surely" text. What you hold in your hands is more of a "get rich fairly quickly" book. One could label its character "get rich *sort of* quickly, but almost surely." I hope that is good enough. It has been for me and others who have applied the book's philosophy and methods.

One other promise I make to you is this: The content you are about to encounter is my effort to deliver an important message in a way that is at least moderately entertaining for most audiences. Believe it or not, this book offers, among other things, the *lighter side* of personal financial gain (which should help to offset the 10% or so of the material that may read more like a textbook. Given the serious subject matter, that's not bad, is it?) What I intend to do, in other words, is not only guide you to a prosperous destination via an alternative route, but provide an enjoyable trip along the way. Let's get started.

Chapter 2

Case Histories:
You, Too, Could Do This

Now I need to prove to you that what I have asserted, declared, and promised is really possible. That's easy. All I have to do is report a couple of case histories I am personally familiar with to demonstrate the *possibility* of my claim. (Even one case of getting rich without making a lot of money would be sufficient to show that it is possible. How common this apparent economic magic becomes is partly up to you, reader.)

I *could* just cite some hypothetical (but valid) mathematical examples of gaining great wealth on surprisingly low income. For instance, did you know that you can become a millionaire on just $2.74 a day? That is true. Just save $2.74 per day in a tax-deferred account such as an IRA (individual retirement account) or annuity, investing in U.S. stocks. Then all you have to do is keep the money there for 40 years, assuming the average stock market return (12.6% since 1950), and you will have over a million dollars. Alternatively, for simplicity, just save and deposit $1000 a year, or $83.33 a month, or $100 ten times a year, and it adds up to the same thing. If 40 years seems too long to wait, as it does to me, this plan would leave you with $100,000 after about 21 years and nearly half a million after 34 years.[1] Still too long, though, isn't it?

Other examples: A 20-year-old person who puts $2000 a year into an 8%-earning traditional IRA for five years, and then *stops saving*, will have acquired $275,000 at age 65. The total would be over $600,000 at a return of 10%. At 12%, millionaire-hood would be achieved by age 63.[2] Or if you put the $2000 annually in an IRA for only ten years beginning at age 18, and save no more, you will have over a million dollars by age 58 (again assuming the normal 12.6% stock market return).[3] There is nothing complicated about any of this. It is all very mechanical, straightforward, and routine—but *relentless*, fortunately for you.

Another interesting lesson comes from a classic article in *The Wall Street Journal*:

Any American currently earning $10,000 a year pays $23.85 a week, or $1,240 a year, into Social Security. Imagine that, beginning at age 20, you invest that $23.85 a week at market rates. When you retire at age 65, you'll be a millionaire (before inflation). All that on *less than the minimum wage*[4] (italics added).

These examples are all worthy and informative, but we don't want to wait 30 or 40 years to get rich, do we? You can get rich much more quickly *if you make a lot of money*, of course, but our objective is getting rich *without* earning a lot. This book is aimed at those who don't, and won't, make a very high income, and that is most people. So we need some real-life examples of real people getting rich much more rapidly, and without making very much money, of course. I will provide such examples now.

The first case illustration is that of my own parents. Table 2-1 displays the gross income of my parents for each year between 1972 and 2000, inclusive, as taken from their federal income tax returns for the period. As can readily be seen, Mom and Dad made a decent living (they only had one child to support and that support was mostly ended by the period shown) but obviously would still be in the very moderate income category. The highest combined annual income they ever earned up until their retirement in 1975 was $26,352. My father worked for the American Bridge division of U.S. Steel for 43 years (and tells me he hated every minute of it), beginning as a laborer but as a self-taught draftsman and structural engineer for most of that time. My mother did clerical/secretarial work in the late 1940's, was a bookkeeper for our local weekly newspaper for a few years in the '50s and early '60s, and then taught second grade at a Catholic elementary school from 1962 until 1975. Her starting annual teacher's salary was $2,340. I believe this background adequately establishes my parents' credentials as members of that group of people who do not "make a lot of money."

However, also note that my parents' income remained nearly constant, after declining initially, after retirement. This phenomenon has been due to Social Security and pension payments and some very wise, prudent, and conservative investing. (Is this a great country or what?) Our family needed every bit of my parents' financial acumen because of an unfortunate circumstance, and this leads us to a brief digression.

As late as 1970-75 my parents had practically no savings other than the value of their home. My maternal grandfather had always advised my parents *not* to save because he and his wife, my mother's stepmother,

TABLE 2-1

INCOME HISTORY, CASE #1

1972	$21,985.17	1982	$22,934.89	1992	$23,391.00
1973	22,815.59	1983	19,799.14	1993	23,766.00
1974	26,351.66	1984	21,733.24	1994	26,842.00
1975	25,912.70	1985	31,380.00	1995	30,954.00
1976	12,211.98	1986	27,972.30	1996	38,615.00
1977	13,153.47	1987	25,895.92	1997	42,795.60
1978	15,589.37	1988	22,447.00	1998	32,207.72
1979	13,640.11	1989	24,466.00	1999	43,624.67
1980	22,665.50	1990	24,400.00	2000	31,610.75
1981	24,324.90	1991	24,235.00		

Source: Total Income line-item of federal 1040 income tax form. Excluded, therefore, is a portion of post-retirement Social Security payments beginning in 1975. A very small amount of tax-exempt income may also be excluded in some early years.

Author had intended to obtain back copies of 1946-71 returns from the IRS, but is way too cheap and decided not to spend the money. It would have cost $14 per year, $364 in total.

were very well-off and it was assumed that my mother would eventually inherit a substantial sum. However, because of an error in estate planning, this did not occur upon the deaths of my grandfather and his wife. The details of this episode, this intergenerational financial planning lapse, are actually somewhat fascinating and instructive, and will be reported to you later. For now, the relevant point is that my parents were without any real nest egg only a few years before their retirement, did not earn a high income (by any conventional definition of high income), and yet within a very few years were to become reasonably wealthy. The figures I am about to show you demonstrate this and also dramatize a more important reality: how *rapidly* you can get rich without making very much money.

TABLE 2-2 (a-m)
Net Worth History, Case #1

(a) June 17, 1979

Common stock	$25,895.00
U.S. government bonds	61,500.00
Bank accounts & CDs	73,798.00
Receivable (from author)	3,000.00
Life insurance cash value	3,350.00
	$168,543.00

(b) December 25, 1981

Common stock	$33,150.63
U.S. government bonds	61,500.00
Bank accounts & CDs	100,811.62
Life insurance cash value (est.)	4,350.00
	$199,812.25

(c) December 31, 1982

Common stock	$25,749.00
U.S. government bonds	61,500.00
Bank accounts & CDs	117,950.82
Life insurance cash value (est.)	4,350.00
	$209,549.82

(d) September 1985

Common stock	$24,511.87
U.S. government bonds	111,500.00
Other bonds, notes	40,000.00
Annuity	25,000.00
Bank accounts	8,846.19
Life insurance cash value	5,800.00
Real estate—residence	60,000.00
	$275,658.06

(e) December 1987

Common stock	$25,377.00
U.S. government bonds	103,500.00
Muni bonds & bond funds	50,000.00
Annuity	27,516.04
Bank accounts	42,000.00
Life insurance cash value (est.)	5,800.00
Real estate—residence (est.)	65,000.00
	$319,193.04

(f) August 1989

Common stock	$26,818.87
U.S. government bonds	103,500.00
Muni bonds & bond funds	87,385.57
Annuity	31,523.62
Bank accounts	15,651.78
Life insurance cash value (est.)	5,800.00
Real estate—residence (est.)	75,000.00
	$345,679.84

(g) July 6, 1991

Common stock	$21,013.75
U.S. government bonds	103,500.00
Muni bonds & bond funds	125,286.52
Annuity	37,434.58
Bank accounts	22,539.52
Life insurance cash value (est.)	5,800.00
Real estate—residence (est.)	75,000.00
	$390,574.37

(h) April 10, 1993

Common stock	$21,332.26
U.S. government bonds	114,060.00
Muni bonds & bond funds	110,934.96
Annuity	42,144.21
Bank accounts	55,201.24
Life insurance cash value	8,702.17
Real estate—residence (est.)	100,000.00
	$452,374.84

(i) June 20, 1994

Common stock	$19,359.02
U.S. government bonds	107,120.00
Muni bonds & bond funds	91,221.11
Annuity (est.)	47,000.00
Bank accounts	96,993.15
Life insurance cash value	8,928.70
Real estate—residence (est.)	100,000.00
	$470,621.98

(j) January 19, 1996

Common stock	$20,051.00
Bonds & notes	162,575.00
Bond & money market funds	96,244.92
Annuity (est.)	52,000.00
Bank accounts & CD	76,605.48
Life insurance cash value	9,281.88
Real estate—residence (est.)	100,000.00
	$514,758.28

(k) January 4, 1998

Cash & equivalent (bank accts, money mkt. fund)	$212,629.61
Fixed income (bonds & notes, funds, annuity)	303,877.75
Common stock	31,809.38
Life insurance cash value	9,783.04
	$558,099.78

(l) July 15, 1999

Cash & equivalent (bank accts, money mkt. fund)	$162,308.59
Fixed income (bonds & notes, funds, annuity)	312,912.88
Common stock	30,951.89
Real estate—residence (at cost)	88,762.03
Life insurance cash value	10,906.15
	$605,841.54

(m) January 1, 2001

Cash & equivalent	$56,050.70
Fixed income (bonds)	413,374.49
Annuity	68,987.22
Common stock	26,427.39
Real estate—residence (at cost)	89,385.46
Life insurance cash value	3,651.58
	$657,876.84

The reported series necessaily ends with the 2001 entry for comparability with the example to follow. A corollary benefit of this time limit is a compact two decade (approximately) perspective.

Tables 2-2(a) through 2-2(m), and Figure 2.1, show my parents' net worth at various intervals between 1979 and 2001, actually reproducing the inventories of financial holdings we had compiled periodically. (I strongly recommend keeping such an ongoing "scorecard" of wealth accumulation. Not only is it one of the basic financial records every person should have, but it is a useful and interesting progress report and the practice itself may even become an incentive to continue making progress—of no small importance in the enrichment crusade.)

Noteworthy about the information in these documents are (1) the steady and rapid pace of wealth increase, (2) that there are only assets, no liabilities, in these balance sheets, and (3) the high rate of saving relative to income. As can be seen in Table 2-3, my parents saved an average of $22,760 per year between 1979 and 2001 (21½ years) on gross reported income of $27,575 per year, a (nominal)

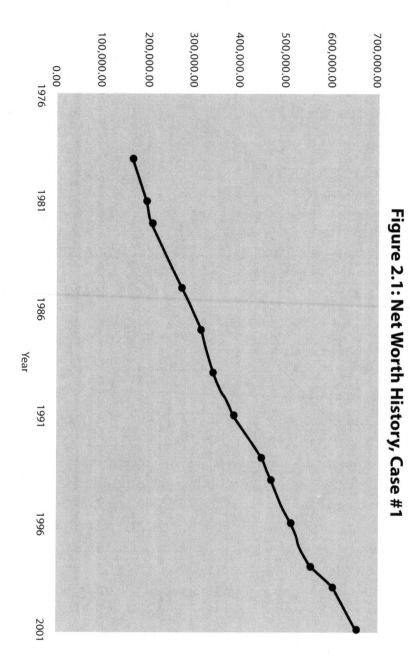

Figure 2.1: Net Worth History, Case #1

saving rate of 82.5%! (Saving is appropriately defined here as total net increment in wealth, including increases in asset values. Moreover, since "income" totals exclude a portion of Social Security payments per IRS rules, it is possible to show a "saving" rate greater than 100%, as reported in some periods. Wealth increase for the 1991-93 interval, for example, also reflects higher appraised value of the residence. Adjusting for such exceptional items and adding-back estimated Social Security payments yields the "adjusted" rates shown in the last column of Table 2-3, and an overall adjusted saving rate of 52%. A conventionally-defined after-tax saving rate cannot be precisely reconstructed, but would be phenomenally high also, somewhere in between the two rates listed.)

What this remarkable record demonstrates is that it is not only possible to get rich without making very much money, but this can be done in a relatively short period of time. Within only four years following their retirement, my parents had accumulated a net worth of over $168,000. After ten years they were worth over $275,000. And in only 16 years (after the 1975 retirement), even at low post-retirement income levels, their personal fortune had grown to about $400,000, all as a result of not spending very much! Not bad for a retired couple in a small town.

Yet I can testify that this phenomenon of high saving, low spending, low income, and rapid wealth accumulation did not come at the price of great hardship. For example, during almost the entire period since they were married in 1945, my parents have belonged to at least one country club (my father remains an avid and expert golfer to this day), two clubs for about half the period. They also were able to send their son to some rather expensive private schools. Our family's life-style was definitely no less than middle- to upper-middle-class throughout (on lower-middle-class income). The point is that *getting rich without making a lot of money* not only can be done fairly quickly, but it can be done *easily*, without suffering deprivation. I know, because my parents did it and so did I.

TABLE 2-3

Example of Wealth Accumulation, Case #1

Time Interval	Increase in Wealth	Income[1]	Annual Saving Rate[2]	Adjusted Rate[3]
6/79 - 12/81 (2 1/2 yrs.)	$31,269.25	$53,810.46	58%	40%
12/81 - 12/82 (1 yr.)	9,737.57	22,934.89	42%	29%
12/82 - 9/85 (2 3/4 yrs.)	66,108.24	65,067.38	102%	70%
9/85 - 12/87 (2 1/4 yrs.)	43,534.98	61,713.22	71%	43%
12/87 - 8/89 (1 2/3 yrs.)	26,486.80	38,757.67	68%	29%
8/89 - 7/91 (1 5/6 yrs.)	44,894.53	44,672.83	100%	69%
7/91 - 4/93 (1 3/4 yrs.)	61,800.47	41,450.00	149%	61%
4/93 - 6/94 (1.2 yrs.)	18,247.14	31,245.50	58%	40%
6/94 - 1/96 (1 1/2 yrs.)	44,136.30	44,375.00	99%	68%
1/96 - 1/98 (2 yrs.)	43,341.50	81,410.60	53%	42%
1/98 - 7/99 (1 1/2 yrs.)	47,741.76	54,020.06	88%	62%
7/99 - 1/01 (1 1/2 yrs.)	52,035.30	53,423.09	97%	72%

[1] Estimated, based on allocation of annual income from Table 2-1 to each time period. For example, 6/79 - 12/81 income includes 50% of 1979 income and all income from 1980-81.
[2] Computed as Increase in Wealth *divided by* Income.
[3] Adjusts for estimated Social Security income (exact figures for each period not available) and exceptional asset gains.

Table 2-4 presents my own annual income totals for most of my adult "working" life. Once again, I believe this establishes a case history of less than high income for most of the time period covered, extremely so in the early years, and some explanation is in order here. The explanation may even provide some amusement.

I got my MBA (Master of Business Administration) degree from Notre Dame in 1973, after having gone to school there as an undergraduate also. As you may know, an MBA degree is generally considered to be a ticket to a high-paying job and an avenue into a successful business career. As a new MBA grad, I had somewhat unconventional motives, however. In seeking employment, which I did rather casually, I had a strong geographic preference. I was anticipating a good football and basketball season by the N.D. Fighting Irish teams and I wanted to find a job in the South Bend, Indiana area (Notre Dame's location) so I would be in a position to attend all the games conveniently. Really! That was the eccentric, frivolous orientation and level of motivation I had at that time. Come to think of it, the main reason I stayed at school for my MBA graduate studies in the first place was that it was the easiest way I could think of to continue to enjoy the wild and crazy life of being a university student. Having a full scholarship to the MBA program made the decision all the more definite. (I had done reasonably well academically as an undergrad but scored very high on the national graduate aptitude test. I have always thought it a mark of efficiency that I received my bachelor's degree with the *minimum* grade point average necessary to be considered an "honor student," i.e., *cum laude* or "with honors." What that signifies, I suppose, is that I put forth the bare minimum effort, did not study one more minute than necessary, to achieve honor status. I do derive satisfaction from that, as I believe in doing things the easy way. That is a theme I will adhere to in this tutorial.)

Back to the story: So after turning down what most people would consider superior job offers in other geographic localities, I found a job in South Bend as "retail marketing director" for a small company in the photo processing business, of all things. As my résumé later described it:

INTERSTATE COLOR LABORATORIES, INC.,
South Bend, Indiana (1973-74)
Retail Marketing Director
Responsible for all marketing activities associated with 20 retail stores in Indiana, Illinois, and Michigan for $3 million firm in the retail and mail order photo processing business.

TABLE 2-4
AUTHOR'S INCOME HISTORY, CASE #2

1973-4	$3,432.73	1987	$61,392.79
1975	6,812.40	1988	60,947.53
1976	6,084.00	1989	68,790.08
1977	5,177.93	1990	73,793.07
1978	6,582.35	1991	79,369.53
1979	8,611.43	1992	82,491.77
1980	22,404.50	1993	79,375.55
1981	29,748.28	1994	85,888.45
1982	34,284.45	1995	86,280.48
1983	37,921.70	1996	88,602.57
1984	40,560.25	1997	95,703.84
1985	41,265.02	1998	94,877.73
1986	45,738.97	1999	95,940.31
		2000	99,218.83

Source: Total Income line item from federal tax returns, including tax-exempt and other investment income; annual salary somewhat lower, in fact never exceeded $80-85,000 during the period.

The reported series ends with the Y2000 entry, of necessity, because after that time the author's income increased beyond the level definable as "without making very much money." That tends to happen after one gets rich on this program. In other words, once a critical mass of wealth is attained, income accelerates.

What did I actually do in that position? Not much. The job paid an annual salary—if I had been there that long—of $10,500! Even in 1973 that compensation level was abysmal, decidedly at the low end of the starting salary range for MBA graduates. (Fortunately, living expenses in South Bend were, and are, very low. Table 2-5 itemizes my personal expenses for the period of my first real job, as recorded by me, in my own hand, at the time.)

But, as I mentioned, my primary interest then was prolonging the party of hanging around my alma mater (and my favorite bars) and watching our sports teams—not very complicated at all. (As I explain to my students now, back then I was purely a leisure maximizer.) In 1973 the Notre Dame football team went undefeated and won the national championship, and the '73-'74 basketball team had a won-lost record of 26-3, so mission accomplished!

That first job out of school only lasted about four months, though. The owner of the company I worked for was preparing to sell the business and eliminated a number of recently-created, non-essential positions for "window dressing" to reduce the payroll and, therefore, make the firm appear more attractive to prospective buyers. Obviously I was regarded as non-essential because I was one of those who got the axe. So as of early 1974, within days of my 25th birthday, I was suddenly out of a job and thus began one of the better times of my life, as a matter of fact. Rather than a setback, I considered it a rare stroke of good fortune to be temporarily, if involuntarily, *retired* at a young age, not having to get up and go to work in the morning, and with enough money to spend—for awhile. I didn't even start looking for a new job for several months. Let's party! (How in the world could I have saved up enough to have spending money even "for awhile" on such a low salary? That secret will be revealed in the coming chapters but an inkling may be found in the extremely low spending categories of Table 2-5. A serious lesson masquerading as the table's "recreation" category is that low spending, high saving, and wealth accumulation can be achieved without sacrificing one's lifestyle. I'm also not too proud to admit that I did collect unemployment compensation and

TABLE 2-5

MONTHLY LIVING EXPENSES: Sept. 1973 - Jan. 1974[1] (Avg. $581.42)

```
1973
 SEPT. 16 - OCT. 15


RENT (INCL. 100⁰⁰ DEPOSIT)              $  280.00

UTILITIES - ELECTRIC (DEP.)     25.00
FOOD (INCL. HOUSEHOLD)          64.16
LAUNDRY                          4.44
TRANSPORTATION: (137.22)
    GAS                         10.70
    PLANE, CAB FARE             74.30
    AUTO REPAIRS                52.22
CLOTHING                         4.42
COMMUNICATION: (2.17)
    POSTAGE                       .32
    NEWSPAPERS                  1.85
RECREATION:
  (BEER, POOL, CIGARETTES, ETC., INCL.  95.94
   $6⁰⁰ IN FOOTBALL BETS)
                                $  613.35


  NOV. 16 - DEC. 15

RENT                            $  135.00
UTILITIES - ELECTRIC               5.42
FOOD                              73.03
HOUSEHOLD                           .94
LAUNDRY                            1.95
TRANSPORTATION:
    GAS                 8.00
    BUS FARE            1.25
    MIAMI TRIP        160.00
    PARKING FINE        1.00      170.25
COMMUNICATION:
    PHONE             10.91
    POSTAGE             .16
    NEWSPAPERS         2.45        13.52

CHRISTMAS EXPENSE, DONATIONS, ETC.  26.43
RECREATION:
  SPORTS-
    ADMISSIONS         1.50
    PROGRAMS           3.50
    RACE TRACK LOSS   12.00
    OTHER BETS-NET    (1.00)       16.00

  SELF-INDULGENCE -               117.25
                                $  559.79
```

TABLE 2-5 continued...

Oct. 16 - Nov. 15

	$
RENT	135.00
UTILITIES- ELECTRIC	5.20
FOOD	85.25
HOUSEHOLD	4.26
CLOTHING (TUXEDO RENTAL)	26.50
LAUNDRY	5.09
TRANSPORTATION: (16.35)	
GAS	5.00
CAR FARE	3.25
PARKING	8.10
COMMUNICATION: (42.97)	
PHONE	39.01
POSTAGE	2.16
NEWSPAPERS	1.80
RECREATION:	
SELF-INDULGENCE —	
(BEER, POOL, CIGARETTES, ETC.)	117.44
MISCELLANEOUS DISCRETIONARY	6.12
	$ 444.18

Dec. 16 - Jan. 15, 1974

	$
RENT	135.00
UTILITIES - ELECTRIC	5.34
FOOD	53.94
HOUSEHOLD	2.09
LAUNDRY	.65
TRANSPORTATION:	
GAS	23.80
CAB FARE	3.40
AIR TRAVEL	112.91
PARKING	.50
AUTO MAINTENANCE	36.35
COMMUNICATION:	
PHONE	10.24
POSTAGE	2.00
NEWSPAPERS	1.50
CHRISTMAS GIFTS	174.74
RECREATION:	
SPORTS —	
ADMISSIONS	4.50
PROGRAMS	1.50
MAGAZINES	1.24
N.D. BOOKSTORE	4.11
NET BETS (2.00)	9.35
SELF-INDULGENCE	136.55
	$ 708.36

TABLE 2-5 continued...

[1] Table is reproduced from author's own records compiled at the time. Some categories listed may be informative because of the non-spending capability they demonstrate, and some may be downright comical. Yes, the author really did use the term "self-indulgence" in financial records, with the accompanying description leaving little to the imagination.

food stamps for a short time, so to all those in similar undignified straits, take heart! It can be done.)

Of course, being out of work for a few months makes it more difficult to get a job, as potential employers begin to wonder why you've been idle for so long. (I didn't think much about that, or anything else, at the time because I wasn't very career-oriented, to say the least. Such extended adolescence was actually fairly common among my generation.) Ultimately, I was unemployed for about a year before I took a job as a salesman for a distributor of institutional laundry machinery (again, of all things). As I told people at the time, "The short job description is that I sell washing machines. The long description is that I sell *great big* washing machines." The actual job description from my actual résumé is this:

L & S EQUIPMENT, INC.,
Fort Wayne, Indiana (1975-76)
Salesman
Sold heavy-duty laundry machinery to institutions such as hospitals, nursing homes, hotels, motels, schools, industrial plants, and restaurants for industrial distributor with annual sales of approximately $1 million.

Oh yes, and I took a pay cut for that job! The salary was even lower than in my previous position, starting at $150 a week while in training, and then never more than $200 per week up until I went on straight commission. Altogether I earned about $10,000 in a *year and a half* on that job, yet I consider it to have been a satisfactory experience. Again, because of my very unusual motives and job criteria, I had a terrific time during that period. Because my sales territory was in a different part of the state from our small company's headquarters, I had nearly total freedom over my own activities and schedule. I managed to sell enough to keep my boss happy, or at least placated. Some weeks I worked five days, some weeks I worked five hours, and some weeks I worked five minutes. During the summer I played golf whenever I felt like it, which was frequently—still the leisure maximizer. A 26-year-old punk, as I was, could have had it a lot worse. I certainly never wanted to be a salesman. Actually, the only reason I did it at all was that I had been given assurance the job would evolve into a management position, which never occurred (maybe my boss wasn't as satisfied as I thought), but it wasn't all bad by any means. And I never was short of money despite the remarkably low compensation. A sample of relevant living expenses, again from my records, appears as Table 2-6. Even today as a college professor, some of my experiences in the hard-knocks real world of industrial selling provide examples for my students. I'll never forget the time I sold a large installation to a Holiday Inn managed by a friend of mine, only to have the equipment set fire to and burn up the laundry room the first day it was in operation! Had to have a few beers after that one. Sorry.

Thus the explanation for the extraordinarily low income levels of the 1973-76 period in Table 2-4. The explanation for 1976-80 is that I was finally getting more serious and had returned to graduate school to get a doctorate, this time at the University of Wisconsin, and was living on the low annual stipend paid for part-time service as a research assistant (1976-77), teaching assistant (1977-79), and lecturer (1979-80). My total stipend for the 1976-77 school year was $4000; $6000 annually for the next two academic years. Then I made the *really big money*, $15,000, during my final year as a Ph.D. student when I had the job of lecturer. That means I taught two classes per semester instead of one, which was the load for a teaching assistant. (Slight discrepancies from reported income per Table 2-4 are attributable to other minor sources of income. Also be mindful of the divergence between the academic year and the calendar year.)

TABLE 2-6

TYPICAL MONTHLY LIVING EXPENSES, 1975 (Average $661.38)

SEPTEMBER

		#
RENT		125.00
FOOD		69.16
HOUSEHOLD		6.33
DRY CLEANING		3.35
MEDICAL		13.00
TELEPHONE		11.90
POSTAGE		.25
NEWSPAPER		.15
AUTO :		
MAINTENANCE	14.93	
TIRES	167.68	
PARKING*	2.80	
TOLLS	10.35	195.76
TIPS		2.71
TAVERN EXPENSE :		
BEER	138.15	
POOL	4.35	
OTHER AMUSEMENTS	1.50	
OTHER BEVERAGES	6.80	150.80
CIGARETS		14.55
SPORTS : *		
ADMISSIONS	5.00	
PROGRAMS	1.50	
PUBLICATIONS	3.38	9.88

		#
(GAS ALLOC^N: 53.54)		602.84
INCL. GAS, OIL	96.89	$ 699.73
LESS : MILEAGE	173.40	$ 526.33

$ 656.38

' INCL. PERSONAL USE GAS & OIL ALLOCATION.

So why am I telling you, and possibly boring you, with all this about my own sordid personal history?—to demonstrate that even a young, wayward, irresponsible slacker is capable of getting rich within only a few short years, easily, and without making very much money! So if you are doubting your own capability to achieve the apparent financial miracle I am offering you, you are probably wrong. You *can* do it. I did it, and if I, the shiftless kid I have described, can do it, almost anybody can.

One thing you will have noticed by now is that I did not exactly get an early start on the process of getting rich without making very much money. Oh, I was attending to the "without making very much money" part all along, but as late as 1980 (age 31) I still had minimal wealth (panel *f* of Table 2-7's wealth progression), as I was just getting out of school with my doctorate.

The expense records from the 1976-80 graduate school period dramatize a very serious and legitimate principle, nevertheless (see illustrative Table 2-8). That is, how little money you absolutely need to spend if you really try to keep expenditures down. From the table, and several others just like it but not shown (to spare you), my average monthly spending bill through four years at the U. of Wisconsin was $534, a mere $468 not counting tuition. I believe the most striking and remarkable financial feat of this period was that even during the time when I was barely making scratch, only $4000-6000 in annual salary, my net wealth actually *increased* slightly each year (see Tables 2-7b to 2-7f). This also is the reason I have so little sympathy for those who claim they are unable to save any money, or can't make ends meet. If I can put money away on a salary of $4000 a year (about $9000 in 2008 dollars), almost anyone can save money.

The post-1980 period, during which time I actually have had a real job (if you consider what a college professor does a real job), also demonstrates an extraordinary saving performance. Though I have earned a respectable salary by college professor standards (see Table 2-4), my income level throughout the period still would have to be considered within the moderate range. Note that my average annual income over

TABLE 2-7 (a-y): Net Worth History, Case #2

(a) Jan. 2, 1975

Common stock	$1,005.00
Bonds	6,000.00
Cash/bank accounts	410.52
	$7,415.52

(b) Jan. 1, 1976

Common stock	$1,410.00
Bonds	6,000.00
Cash/bank accounts	2,819.29
	$10,229.29

(c) Jan. 1, 1977

Common stock	$2,085.00
Bonds	9,000.00
Bank accounts	6,593.65
	$17,678.65

(d) Jan. 1, 1978

Common stock	$1,830.00
Bonds	9,000.00
Bank accounts	6,956.84
	$17,786.84

(e) Jan. 13, 1979

Common stock	$1,852.50
Bonds	10,000.00
Bank accounts	6,943.02
	$18,795.52

(f) Aug. 20, 1980

Common stock	$2,062.50
Fixed income: notes	16,822.81
Bank accounts	5,560.96
	$24,446.27

(g) Feb. 1, 1983

Common stock	$2,464.50
Fixed income: note	14,211.24
Cash & equivalent (bank account, money market funds)	33,479.15
	$50,154.89

(h) Feb. 1, 1984

Common stock	$2,638.88
Fixed income: note	16,369.81
Cash & equivalent	44,667.43
Retirement annuity	9,616.74
	$73,292.86

(i) April 1, 1985

Common stock	$2,673.75
Fixed income: bond funds, note	70,034.93
Cash & equivalent	14,034.04
Retirement annuity	14,928.37
	$101,671.09

(j) March 13, 1986

Common stock	$2,662.12
Bond mutual funds	97,674.51
Cash & equivalent	15,952.97
Retirement annuity	23,517.82
	$139,807.42

(k) March 12, 1987

Common stock	$2,731.88
Bank account	6,536.10
Bond mutual funds	137,590.93
Retirement annuity	33,190.59
	$180,049.50

TABLE 2-7 (a–y) continued...

(l) Feb. 1, 1988

Cash & equivalent	$133,200.47
Bond mutual fund	17,802.80
Retirement annuity	41,651.52
	$192,654.79

(m) Feb. 1, 1989

Cash & equivalent	$154,069.80
Bond, bond funds	25,789.94
Partnership interests–	
investment club	243.34
Retirement annuity	54,602.08
	$234,705.16

(n) Feb. 1, 1990

Cash & equivalent	$181,708.90
Muni bond, bond fund	29,895.50
Partnership interests	3,599.25
Retirement annuity	73,495.04
	$288,698.69

(o) Feb. 1, 1991

Cash & equivalent	$214,519.25
Muni bond, bond fund	34,847.52
Partnership interests–	
investment club &	
bar/night club	4,984.59
Retirement annuity	82,644.36
	$336,995.72

(p) Feb. 1, 1992

Cash & equivalent	$289,115.18
Partnership interests	4,049.28
Retirement annuity	109,193.87
	$402,358.33

(q) Feb. 1, 1993

Cash & equivalent	$328,137.61
Common stock	
(regional banks)	64,261.04
Retirement annuity	127,253.54
	$519,652.19

(r) Feb. 1, 1994

Cash & equivalent	$280,557.90
Common stock	76,815.48
Real estate–residence	85,217.56
Retirement annuity	152,340.10
	$594,931.04

(s) Feb. 1, 1995

Cash & equivalent	$289,950.85
Muni bond	25,000.00
Common stock	74,173.79
Real estate–residence	
(at cost)	85,808.31
Retirement annuity	167,770.36
	$642,703.31

(t) Feb. 1, 1996

Cash & equivalent	$336,028.15
Muni bond	25,000.00
Common stock	106,022.51
Real estate–residence	
(at cost)	85,933.18
Retirement annuity	215,273.99
	$768,257.83

TABLE 2-7 (a-y) continued...

(u) Feb. 1, 1997

Cash & equivalent	$384,462.06
Muni bond	25,500.00
Common stock	148,481.73
Real estate—residence (at cost)	86,839.97
Retirement annuity	263,796.04
	$909,079.80

(v) Feb. 1, 1998

Cash & equivalent	$408,155.36
Fixed income: muni bond, preferred stock	57,600.00
Common stock	228,904.88
Real estate—residence (at cost)	87,051.68
Retirement annuity	331,558.42
	$1,113,270.34

(w) Feb. 1, 1999

Cash & equivalent	$459,368.58
Fixed income	56,175.00
Common stock	264,803.91
Real estate—residence (at cost)	87,325.47
Retirement annuity	406,971.31
	$1,274,644.27

(x) Feb. 1, 2000

Cash & equivalent	$431,592.19
Fixed income	136,676.02
Common stock	211,803.84
Real estate—residence (at cost)	87,557.24
Retirement annuity	495,268.08
	$1,362,897.37

(y) Feb. 1, 2001

Cash & equivalent	$446,742.68
Fixed income	201,019.26
Common stock	221,076.61
Real estate—residence (at cost)	88,202.29
Retirement annuity	497,800.54
	$1,454,841.38

The reported series necessarily ends with the 2001 entry for reasons explained in Table 2-4, i.e., after that time income increased beyond the level definable as "without making very much money." Correspondingly, the net worth numbers of more recent years, not shown, are also much larger, their growth accelerating too. Readers could experience the same.

One corollary benefit of this time limitation is a tidy quarter-century-or-so perspective.

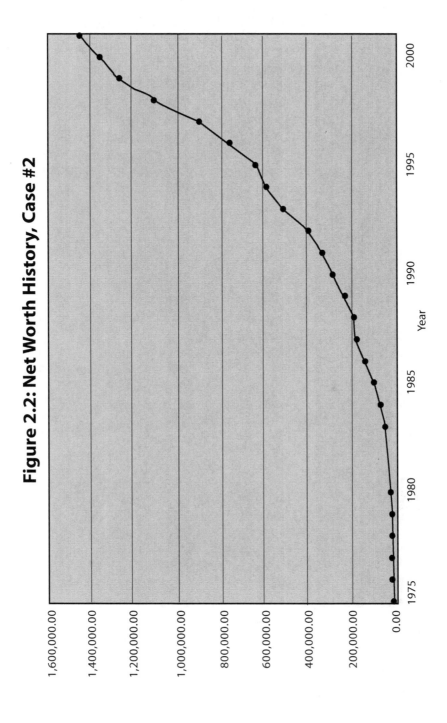

Figure 2.2: Net Worth History, Case #2

TABLE 2-8   **TYPICAL MONTHLY LIVING EXPENSES, 1976-80**

JUNE 1977		JULY 1977		AUGUST 1977	
Rent-parking	$95.00	Rent-parking	$95.00	Rent-parking	$140.00
Phone	7.65	Phone	17.17	Phone	5.87
Groceries	14.36	Groceries	47.59	Groceries	13.57
Electric	6.61	Electric	11.83	Electric	(26.30)
Meal ticket	73.50	Library fine	8.00	Cash	140.00
Books	37.44	Cash	70.10	Master charge	8.30
Magazines	12.50	Master charge	30.59		**$307.74**
Gas bill	8.11		**$280.28**		
Gifts	23.03				
Cash	140.04				
	$418.60				

SEPT. 1977		OCT. 1977		NOV. 1977	
Rent-parking	$140.00	Rent-parking	$140.00	Rent-parking	$140.00
Phone	7.55	Phone	29.16	Phone	9.38
Groceries	27.18	Groceries	46.64	Groceries	35.49
Electric	(8.48)	Electric ($7.34)	42.12	Electric	5.34
Meal ticket	85.95	Meal ticket	58.60	Copy center	15.00
Books	20.28	Gifts	3.99	Gas	9.50
Tuition		Cash	106.00	Gifts	26.36
(519.-500)	19.00	Master charge	3.20	Cash	125.00
Gifts	5.02		**$429.71**		**$366.07**
Motel	20.00				
Cash	164.40				
	$489.38				

DEC. 1977		JAN. 1978		FEB. 1978	
Rent-parking	$140.00	Rent-parking	$140.00	Rent-parking	$140.00
Phone	13.55	Phone	7.51	Phone	11.66
Groceries	19.83	Groceries	31.67	Groceries	52.15
Electric	5.54	Electric	4.00	Electric	2.92
Books	4.16	Meal ticket	95.75	Gas bill	50.36
Copy center	1.35	Books	48.67	Dental	54.00
Gas bill	8.00	Copy center	3.70	Books	14.51
N.D. club dues	10.00	Printing	7.80	Hocky tickets	8.00
N.D. annual fund	25.00	TV repair	25.44	Cash	90.00
Gifts	3.99	Cash	105.00	Master charge	2.21
Cash	171.50	Tuition	519.00		**$425.81**
Master charge	150.00	Master charge	7.60		
	$552.92		**$996.14**		

the 28-year time-frame was only $51,475, which is barely two times the minimal (low-paid laborer) amounts we've considered as exemplary of low income. It also is only about three times the current minimum wage, a level which one of our two main political parties regards as destitute enough for federal assistance! (My average income level, that is, not minimum wage itself.) Thus, I qualify as not having made "very much money."

Yet Table 2-9 shows a saving rate that averaged *78%* through 1996. In fact, the saving rates listed are so high as to be beyond belief. In some years, the savings exceed the total income! How can that be, especially after taxes? It's not magic (or tax evasion), I can assure you. Actually, the "Increase in Wealth" column includes the increase in my 403(b) retirement account, as it should, while the income numbers of Table 2-9 do not reflect that gain, as they shouldn't. Also, small inheritance amounts are included in a few years' "wealth increase" entries, though not qualifying as income (mostly about $70,000 in regional bank stocks from Uncle Leo in '93-94). The "Adjusted Saving Rate" column reflects the deletion of such exceptional items (but includes other gains in asset values), and yet is impressive enough in its own right, averaging 51%—though I never earned $100,000 a year until long after I already was rich!

I recall one summer morning during the latter Table 2-9 period (it must have been 1990) when I was driving to the golf course with a visiting college classmate of mine who had since become a highly successful businessman, the chief executive of a medium-sized company. During the course of our conversation on the general subject of how we were doing, my friend revealed that he had saved about $16,000 the previous year on income of $140,000. I then informed him that I had made about $70,000 and saved $54,000! We both got a hearty laugh out of that because it was obviously so typical of my penurious proclivities, which by then were becoming somewhat legendary among the people who knew me. As another of my friends expresses it, "He never buys anything." (Yet I have everything I want, and then some.)

TABLE 2-9

EXAMPLE OF WEALTH ACCUMULATION, CASE #2

Time Interval	Increase in Wealth	Income[1]	Saving Rate[2]	Adjusted Saving Rate
1/75-1/76	$2,813.77	$6,812.40	41%	41%
1/76-1/77	7,449.36[3]	6,084.00	122%	73%
1/77-1/78	108.19	5,177.93	2%	2%
1/78-1/79	1,008.68	6,582.35	15%	15%
1/79-8/80 (1.5 yrs.)	5,650.75	19,813.68	29%	29%
8/80-2/83 (2.5 yrs.)	25,708.62[4]	75,234.98	34%	34%
2/83-2/84	23,137.97	37,921.70	61%	36%
2/84-4/85	28,378.23	40,560.25	70%	57%
4/85-3/86	38,136.33	41,265.02	92%	72%
3/86-3/87	40,242.08	45,738.97	88%	67%
3/87-2/88	12,605.29	61,392.79	21%	7%
2/88-2/89	42,050.37	60,947.53	69%	48%
2/89-2/90	53,993.53	68,790.08	78%	51%
2/90-2/91	48,297.03	73,793.07	65%	53%
2/91-2/92	65,362.61	79,369.53	82%	49%
2/92-2/93	117,293.86[3]	82,491.77	142%	60%
2/93-2/94	75,278.85[3]	79,375.55	95%	46%
2/94-2/95	47,772.27[3]	85,888.45	56%	33%
2/95-2/96	125,554.52[3]	86,280.48	146%	87%
2/96-2/97	140,821.97	88,602.57	159%	104%
2/97-2/98	204,190.50	95,703.84	213%[5]	143%
2/98-2/99	161,373.97	94,877.73	170%	91%
2/99-2/00	88,253.10	95,940.31	92%	0%[5]
2/00-2/01	91,944.01	99,218.83	93%	90%

[1]Total from closest corresponding calendar year used for simplicity, e.g., 2/83-2/84 period represented by 1983 income from Table 2-4. (Obviously, this simplification slightly understates 2/84-4/85 income and overstates the amount associated with 4/85-3/86, for example.) Income from 1980 allocated equally between 1/79-8/80 and 8/80-2/83 periods.

[2]Calculated as Increase in Wealth *divided by* Income.

[3]Includes some moderate inheritance money. About $3000 of 1976 total due to inheritance from step-grandmother, who had passed away in *1970*—an example of why you want to avoid probate.

[4]1983 total ignores minimal pension fund accumulation, slightly understating '80-'83 gain and overstating '83-'84 gain. Author asks forgiveness for not keeping more precise records at a time when he was working his butt off to publish enough to get tenure.

[5]The post-1995 period includes abnormal gains in the retirement stock account (and one abnormal down year). This, however, does exemplify what gains you can easily achieve once you reach a critical mass of wealth.

Naturally, it is not recommended to discuss personal finances, such as income or net worth-related matters, with other people. I certainly never have except with a very small circle of close friends, fewer than a handful. (Sure, I'll tell everything to the world now, to illustrate the principles contained in this book, but it's all for a noble purpose: your enrichment.) I have to confess, though, that when a colleague once asked me how much I had saved the previous year, I really enjoyed reporting $125,000! Or was it $200,000?

Returning to our central concerns, the claim that I don't buy *anything* is not quite true. Although I was growing tired of periodically recording my cash expenditures day after day for months at a time, I subjected myself to that ritual once more during the February-April 1983 period. (Sorry I don't have anything more recent. I refuse to impose that kind of record-keeping burden on myself ever again, even for my readers.) Table 2-10 therefore shows another moderate pattern of spending even relative to my income level, but one nowhere near the rock-bottom, bare-bones, skinflint tight-fistedness of 1976-80 or before. Inspection of one or two of the recreation-related categories also reveals no shortage of self-indulgence, which in my case was still focused primarily on patronizing my favorite nightspots (pardon me, I mean socializing) and playing golf, in season. Yes, I'm single. As a woman I once dated described me a few years ago (quite a few now): "All you do is play golf every day and go to singles bars every night, and you've hardly worked a day in your life."

TABLE 2-10
MONTHLY LIVING EXPENSES, FEB.-APRIL 1983

```
EXPENDITURES — FEB. 1983

RENT                                    306.00
ELECTRIC                                 86.12
TELEPHONE                                13.02
CABLE TV                                 32.18
FOOD
    GROCERIES                  52.93
    ON-PREMISE                120.69
    TAKE-OUT                    9.06   182.68
HOUSEHOLD/PERSONAL                        8.46
PERS. SERVICES-HAIRCUT                   13.00
AUTO
    GAS                        24.98
    MTCE.-CAR WASH              4.75
    LICENSE PLATES             62.50
    DRIVER'S LICENSE            6.00    98.23
NEWSPAPER                                 7.15
TIPS                                      5.65
GIFTS                                     6.10
PERSONAL BUSINESS
    COPY                        .15
    POSTAGE                    4.00
    BOOKS                     14.00     18.15
PROFESSIONAL BUSINESS
    OFFICE SUPPLIES             .75
    JOURNALS                  20.00     20.75
RECREATION
    DRINKING, NIGHTLIFE, ETC.
        BEER                 102.46
        SOFT DRINKS            3.75    106.21
    PARTY FEE                            12.00
    SPECTATOR SPORTS
        ADMISSION             1.50
        PROGRAMS              3.25
        REFRESHMENTS          3.25      8.00

                                       923.70
```

MAR, 1983

RENT		306.00
ELECTRIC		64.31
TELEPHONE		14.89
CABLE TV		32.18
FOOD		
GROCERIES	83.06	
ON-PREMISE	107.54	
TAKE-OUT	12.93	
VENDING	.40	203.93
HOUSEHOLD/PERSONAL		19.87
AUTO		
GAS	69.15	
MTCE.-OIL CHANGE, LUBE	10.48	79.63
NEWSPAPER		10.20
TIPS		8.30
PERSONAL BUSINESS		
COPY		.05
PROFESSIONAL BUSINESS		
TRAVEL		138.55
RECREATION		
N.D. CLUB DUES		10.00
TRAVEL		
SALT LAKE CITY TRIP	400.00	
MOTEL	33.64	
CAB FARE	14.60	
TOLLS	2.00	450.24
DRINKING, NIGHTLIFE, ETC.		
BEER	137.63	
SOFT DRINKS	1.35	
ICE	2.00	
POOL, PINBALL	5.50	146.48
SPECTATOR SPORTS		
ADMISSION	101.00	
PROGRAMS	2.50	
PARKING	2.00	
REFRESHMENTS	2.00	107.50
UNKNOWN		.75
		1,592.88

APR. 1983

RENT		306.00
ELECTRIC		74.93
TELEPHONE		30.97
CABLE TV		32.18
FOOD		
GROCERIES	34.62	
ON-PREMISE	180.66	
TAKE-OUT	21.10	
VENDING	.80	237.18
HOUSEHOLD/PERSONAL		7.71
AUTO		
GAS	49.50	
MTCE.- CAR WASH	6.25	55.75
NEWSPAPER		11.30
TIPS		9.80
GIFTS		1.31
STATE INCOME TAXES		55.60
PERSONAL BUSINESS		
COPY	.70	
POSTAGE	11.58	
CHECK PRINTING	8.00	
MISC.	9.47	29.75
PROFESSIONAL BUSINESS--BOOKS		22.45
RECREATION		
MARINE CORPS LEAGUE DUES		6.00
AIR TRAVEL		314.00
MOVIE		8.00
DRINKING, ETC.		
BEER	160.45	
SOFT DRINKS	5.85	
POOL, PIN BALL	3.55	169.85
GOLF		
GREENS FEES	15.00	
RANGE	1.75	16.75
SPECTATOR SPORTS		
ADMISSION	3.00	
PROGRAMS	.50	3.50
		1,393.03

I wish. Thanks, but it hasn't been *quite* that easy. And I always thought those places were neighborhood taverns.

One lesson this anecdote does reinforce, emphatically, is how you can still have plenty of fun while on my program of saving money and getting rich. The message to you is how good the thrifty lifestyle can appear to others, and can be in reality. It is precisely because I spend so little in general that I can afford to abide any spending desire that comes along. Because I care nothing for personal possessions like clothing or luxury items, and spend virtually nothing on them, I've also thought nothing of going out on the town, as it were, most any night of my adult life. (Literally, I believe I have spent a majority, i.e., more than half, of my evenings partying, bar-hopping, or otherwise recreating since I was 18 years old—a much higher concentration long ago than in recent years, of course. Nothing radical, just kind of like the *Cheers* routine popularized by my occasional undergrad drinking buddy, actor George Wendt.) The only relevant point I wish to make with this information is, once again, how *easily* one can get rich without making very much money *and without sacrificing life-style*. One with different discretionary spending preferences, such as fine clothes or other material possessions, could easily substitute them for my favorite forms of entertainment. Nonetheless, this penurious pattern and principle (and pathology?) does explain why I can comfortably spend $6000-7000 or so a year on a country club membership, can whimsically own a piece of both a bar-nightclub and a minor league baseball team, and could semi-frivolously buy an ad in our school's football program magazine for $425 (in 1981 dollars) to promote a post-game party. (See Exhibit 2-1. We actually *made* money on that party, as you might guess—though not very much because we spent another $342 on aerial advertising, i.e., the small plane dragging a banner while circling the stadium overhead. Unfortunately, Notre Dame lost the game. By the way, all the music celebrities named in the ad had one thing in common when it appeared in 1981. What was it?)

Conversely, I mentioned that I care nothing about conspicuous possessions such as clothing (which gives rise to observations like "he never

EXHIBIT 2-1, Party Ad

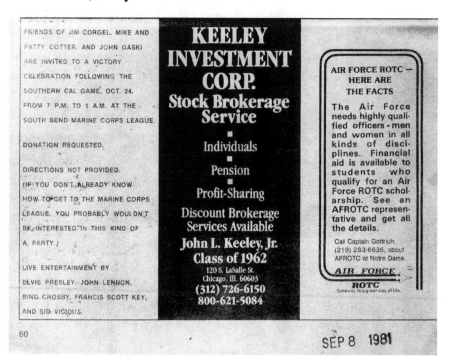

buys anything" and my usual rejoinder of "I'll keep my money in the bank, not on my back.") Please do not be skeptical about the following statement because it is absolutely and literally true. I have never bought an article of clothing in my 50+ years of life other than underwear and shoes, with only *one* exception: a leather overcoat. How? Parents and a few other close relatives generally have given me clothes as Christmas and birthday gifts. Aside from generosity, my parents' primary motive may be fear of what their son's appearance will be if they don't. I have also received many hand-me-downs that Mom tailored, and I usually select clothing when I win merchandise in golf events. Much of my wardrobe is 25-30 years old or more (polyester forever!) and, with any luck, in five years it will be 30-35 years old. I actually still have a few items that I wore in college.

If this approach to saving money and getting rich does not appeal to you, fine. Go ahead and substitute new clothing for going out carousing almost every night. But by now the principle should be evident: You can have fun, you can indulge yourself, you can have luxuries, or you can have physical accoutrements, *and* you can get rich without making a lot of money. But you do have to choose. You cannot have *all* of the above. You have to be selective about what to allow yourself if you want to get rich without making very much money. (If you do wish to have "all of the above," then you need to make some money.) As I have demonstrated, though, and as I have lived it, you certainly do not have to deprive yourself.

Now, as you can imagine, the large "oldies" segment of my wardrobe is a source of great amusement to my friends and acquaintances. I receive my share of jokes about polyester. My standard response is this: Anyone who gives a damn about fashion is a fool, or at least a lemming. Do you really want to allow a handful of French fashion designers to control your behavior? Oh, I would be glad to discard all my vintage 1970's polyester—if you are willing to buy me replacement clothes. I will be very content to throw away those old garments when they wear out. (Sometimes my mother compels me to do that.) The trouble is, that polyester stuff almost never wears out.

Truly, I have nothing but contempt for fashion and its adherents (a highly useful attitude if you want to save money, so I suggest its adoption by you), and I am sure the fashion world is perfectly at ease with that separation between us. Very seriously, though, if fancy clothes are important to you, so be it. That tendency, if managed within reason, will not necessarily prevent you from the success I promise, although it could. But think it over. Are new clothes really as important as getting rich? Wouldn't you rather be rich? Get rich first and then you can buy all the clothes you want.

Incidentally, I have never purchased an automobile either. My unusual car ownership history goes like this: My first car was a 1965 Plymouth Belvidere, given to me by an uncle in 1972 when I was in grad school. (If it is beginning to seem like I was a "professional student," I guess I was for awhile. I spent a total of 11 1/2 years in college and graduate school, with only the conventional four as an undergrad. I like to think I may actually know something about money after having studied business for so long. I have a bachelor's degree in marketing, an MBA in management, an M.S. in finance, and a Ph.D. in business with a major in marketing and minors in finance and economics at the doctoral level—just in case anyone wanted to check my formal credentials.) In 1975 when I took the job selling laundry machinery (!) and moved out of my folks' house, finally, at age 26, my parents gave me my mother's 1972 Dodge Dart as she was receiving another hand-me-down from my uncle. While I was working on my doctorate in the late 1970's, my father told me that if I ever got a real job he would give me his car, a very fine 1977 Buick Electra 225. (Obviously my father was conscious of my long-term reluctance to put myself to work, and thought I needed an incentive.) Apparently Dad considered the condition to have been met when I joined a university faculty, and gave me his "deuce and a quarter" (with only 20,000 miles on it) in the fall of 1980 as he traded my Dart in on his new car. This scenario was repeated, more or less, when my father bought a new car in 1988, for which he traded in my Electra, and gave me his 1985 Buick LeSabre, again in '92 when I got his '88 Park Avenue, and again in '97 when I got the '92. (Technically, these "gifts" were transactions at a price of "$1 and other considerations.") The most recent trade gave me a '97 LeSabre in Y2002, which I still drive. That is how a now-59-year-old man has never really bought an automobile.

Of course, I couldn't complain about this arrangement and am supremely grateful to my father for his generosity in attending to his only son's automotive needs, as well as practically everything else for so many years. (I've offered to reverse the deal and be the one buying and giving, but my father won't hear of it. Even at age 90-something, my parents are still taking care of their little boy.) Obviously Dad could afford to be so generous because he had practiced the principles outlined in this book, as proven in Tables 2-1 through 2-3. Note also that my father's pattern of sacrifice in trading in his son's old cars instead of his newer ones actually makes my parents' savings record (Table 2-2) even more impressive (and mine slightly less so). In other words, my parents would be worth even more, and I a little less, in the absence of my father's particular brand of generosity.

Perhaps the most meaningful perspective on this is to view my parents and me as a single economic entity. Starting out from practically nothing in the late 1970's, we built wealth of over $700,000 within the course of about a dozen years (half a million within only eight years!), $1.1 million in 15 years, and over $2.1 million in 20 years. You could do the same. Believe me, it wasn't very hard and it has been great fun. (If the saving rates of Tables 2-3 and 2-9 seem unrealistic, as they might, be forewarned that other examples of similar performance will be reported to you later.) And bear in mind that all this was accomplished without full-time employment for most of the period! Now, that aspect *is* unusual. Of the 60 person-years between 1970 and 1990 among the three of us, my parents and I were regularly employed for about 22 of those years (37%) combined. For the 1970-2000 period (90 person-years) the employed years total 32, or 35%.

Marilyn Mach vos Savant, the self-proclaimed "smartest person in the world" (as evidenced by the highest I.Q. score on record), made a very reckless and ignorant statement a few years ago. In answer to a reader's question in her weekly syndicated magazine column, Ms. vos Savant claimed "no one becomes wealthy by saving; people become wealthy by *earning*."[5] I could go on, based on "philosophy of science" principles known to college professors and others of our kind, about how the attempt to assert a universal, unbounded, negative statement is futile and inadmissible. The shorthand, plain English, expression for the surprising error by the self-styled smart columnist is: You can't prove a negative. It is dangerous to try, because an unqualified negative assertion is so easily falsifiable. All you have to do is find one exception, and we've already produced more than that to falsify the claim that "*no one* becomes wealthy by saving." So much for the smartest person on earth. Now you know something she doesn't know, at least about one subject. Better, you also know how to avoid an embarrassing error made by that writer.

I've just burdened you with more than you ever wanted to know about the financial histories of some total strangers. Why? It is from case studies such as the ones described in this chapter that principles emerge—principles of *getting rich easily* that I will be presenting to you in the coming pages.

No, I can't show you how to acquire a billion dollars or even tens of millions of dollars, but I can teach you how to have at least hundreds of thousands of dollars, or more, in a relatively short amount of time— easily, and without *making* very much money, of course. We can begin doing that now.

Chapter 3

The Philosophy and Psychology of Money
OR Having the Right Attitude

I still remember the day it happened. In fact, I can remember vividly the exact moment I got the idea.

It was 1974. I was 25, unemployed, and living at home, i.e., sponging off my parents again, and I was approaching the drive-up window at Citizens Federal Savings & Loan in Crown Point, Indiana one afternoon (I was rarely up in the morning unless you count midnight to 3 A.M.) to withdraw some money from the savings account that I had diligently built up to about $2000 over the course of my young life. I would withdraw about $50 every week or so to keep myself in drinking money, but this time I felt uneasy about it. I thought to myself, "Wait a minute, this isn't right. I shouldn't be taking money *out* of the bank; I should be putting money *in* the bank." Good thinking, John. I decided then and there that, yes, I wanted to be rich but, no, it wasn't going to happen the way I was going about it. I realized that, given my indolent proclivities—I knew I was lazy—I was probably never going to make very much money. Therefore, the only available way for me to become wealthy was to *save* a lot of the money I did make. I was also smart enough to be at least marginally aware of the reality contained in Table 1-1 and the surrounding text, which is, no matter how little a person earns, over time that does represent a great deal of money. I knew very well even then that it was easily possible to get rich by *saving* money, by

45

achieving a high saving rate even with a low income, and that was how I was going to do it. Yes, I was also assuming I would have to get a job of some kind eventually.

What this mundane anecdote illustrates is something I consider a basic principle, a necessary condition underlying the ability to execute my recommended approach to wealth accumulation. It is required that you make a conscious decision. You must affirmatively choose this alternative course of gaining wealth. You have to decide that you are going to do it differently. You must first realize that this method is available and achievable (which you should have done already by virtue of what you have read here), understand that you know something others don't, and make a decision that you are not going to just follow the crowd.

The beauty of all this is that the initial decision is *almost* all there is to it. Make the decision and everything else tends to fall into place. You see, it is not a matter of hoping, or trying, or working, or struggling to get rich without making very much money. Since this outcome is possible, and easily achievable in most cases, you merely need to decide to do it and then let it happen! Accomplishment is at your discretion. The willful decision itself is the key. One idea on one occasion, and a few brief moments of casual reflective thought, have literally been worth many hundreds of thousands of dollars to me (actually millions, now).

Of course, there are some things you can do to facilitate your financial gain task, to make this inherently achievable process even easier for you. There are some ways of thinking and behaving that can *enhance* the degree to which you will get rich without making very much money. But those things follow naturally from having the right perspective, the right attitude, the right philosophy. We will try now to start inculcating the proper wealth-creating attitude by outlining some general philosophical and psychological orientations that may be helpful for you to ponder.

Asceticism and Deferred Gratification

Asceticism is the philosophy, actually incorporating a way of life, characterized by renunciation of physical amenities and comforts, repression of desires, and austerity. Also inherent in the ascetic approach is methodical effort to control "disordered" tendencies (i.e., the absence of such abstinence and self-denial) through application of the mind and will to achieve moderation of desires.[1] Ultimately, the purpose of asceticism is individual liberation, to allow humans to free themselves from dependence on external factors and their own base tendencies. As you may know, there are also some more extreme aspects of the philosophy, including practices such as fasting, virginity or celibacy, silence, penance, all the way up to sackcloth and ashes, flagellation, whips and chains, and self-mutilation.[2]

What does any of this have to do with our financial business at hand? Am I recommending fasting and sackcloth, or whips and chains, as the way to riches? Certainly not, rest assured. That regimen doesn't seem like much fun to me either, and I do believe in fun, lots of it, for you as well as me. Recall that one of our basic themes is gaining wealth easily *without giving up an enjoyable life-style.* So the value of understanding asceticism lies in appreciating and internalizing *some* of its elements and motivations, selectively drawing upon whatever is helpful to us. Obviously, austerity and abstinence can be useful habits to cultivate if one wishes to develop the financially-beneficial quality of *frugality* or thrift, itself another hallmark of asceticism, which contributes directly to our recommended program leading to easy and simple wealth achievement. If one can get along with less in a material sense, and be satisfied and happy, that clearly makes the necessary task of saving money much easier. How does this square with my assurance of easy wealth *without sacrifice*? It is a matter of degree, a matter of proportion: (1) You can sacrifice *temporarily,* for only a few years, until you have built up enough of a personal fortune to have practically anything you want, as shown in the examples of Chapters 1 and 2. As we saw, the process should only take a very few years (and if you have more income, even less). Or (2) you can practice ascetic self-denial relatively *painlessly* by identifying the things you really need and want and eliminating purchase of the non-essentials. (Don't we wish the federal government could learn to do that?) That may take some practice but you can start by eliminating *everything* except what is required for physiological survival, i.e., food and shelter. (Skip clothing. You already have some.) Try that for awhile and then work backwards to include other things that are most important to you, other purchases that are most desired. You will be surprised at how little you really need, how much you can learn to do without—without hardship! Isn't a lifetime of real wealth one of those other things you really want, one of those "purchases" most desired? That is the real prize. That is what you are actually purchasing by *not* purchasing other things.

Are you resisting? Are you thinking, "Oh, I can't do that. I already save as much as I can and it's practically nothing. There is no way I could ever achieve the rapid wealth gain, those numbers, shown in Chapters 1 and 2." Is that what you are thinking? My response is, I'll bet you've never tried it, or tried it the right way, or you wouldn't have invested in this book.

Asceticism is a philosophy that has been found prominently throughout all periods of recorded human history, across all cultures and religions, so there must be something to it. There must be something inherently agreeable or rewarding to many people in the practice of asceticism. As mentioned, it does not appeal much to me, and probably not you. I do not practice it—consciously. I don't deny myself anything that I want. What I do, and what I recommend for you to do, is isolate what is truly important to oneself, what you genuinely need, and strive toward attainment of only those things. Getting rich without making very much money should be among those things, for you or for almost everyone. (Only a small minority makes enough money to get rich while ignoring the principles in this book.) Isn't rapid and easy financial security more important to you than the relatively worthless baubles you expend your hard-earned money on now? Those are the alternatives.

If you become able to focus on what is *most important*, and in turn devote yourself primarily to those most important things, thereby increasing your *saving rate* beyond anything you ever thought possible, ultimately, naturally, and *inevitably* becoming rich without making very much money, then asceticism, via principles we have derived from it, will have proven to be of great value to you. Even if you never think of the idea or the word itself again, ascetic philosophy will have contributed vastly to your financial welfare by way of the practices you are to learn from this book. Your financial liberation, and the personal freedom that follows from it, are the kind of results intended by the philosophy of asceticism from the beginning, of course. At the very least, if you can appreciate the idea of *temporarily* subordinating spending and consumption urges that you know are unhealthy for you in terms of your financial (and spending and consumption) future, then you will have acquired the main attitudinal trait that leads directly to your getting rich quickly. You will be on track because you will be operating, even unknowingly, on the basis of a guideline, a corollary of asceticism, that underlies our primary wealth-creating philosophical perspective: *deferred gratification.*

Once we express our approach in terms of deferred gratification, it connotes more properly the direct relation to our mission of helping you get rich easily and quickly. We certainly do not advocate forgoing gratification from consumption. I never said you should "do without." We are all for you consuming to your heart's content, splurging until you drop, if that's what you want—but only at the right time. It is rather a matter of temporarily postponing consumption and its associated gratification until you can comfortably afford it, until you have built up a critical mass of wealth. Fortunately, if you do it right, do it the way I outline, that will not take long. You know full well that if you blow all your money now on unnecessary consumption, you'll never have *squat*, to put it bluntly. I'm here to prevent you from falling into that common trap. (I believe my record and background qualify me to do that.) If I can do it, myself—if I can actually *save money* on income of $4000-$5000 a year (!), as I once did—you can do it, too. Almost anyone can.

One very positive indication for you is the mere fact that you are reading this right now. That shows you have at least the beginning of the correct mind-set, and maybe more. Welcome to the party.

There is a concept in finance known as *net present value*. Perhaps you are familiar with it. It refers to the current or "present" equivalent value of a *future* payment or income stream. For example, if you were to invest one dollar today at an interest rate of 5% per annum, a year from today you would have a total of $1.05. That $1.05 amount, therefore, is the *future value*, one year hence, of your present dollar, at an interest rate of 5%. And $1.00 is the net *present value* of $1.05 received a year from now, again assuming a rate of 5%.

What the notion of "present value" indicates, then, is that a given amount of future money ($x) is worth less than the same nominal amount *right now*. The reason, of course, is that an amount *less than* $x could be invested, starting right now, to equal $x at the given future time. That is why the lottery winner who receives a million dollars in the form of $50,000 annual payments over a 20-year period is actually receiving much less than a million dollars in *present* value, in any interest rate environment other than 0%.

In other words, the difference between present value (of an amount of money) and its future value is the amount of interest that could have been earned on the original amount over the time interval between the present and the particular future time. Is this because of expected inflation? Only indirectly: Interest is the price of money that people, such as lenders, are willing to receive, and need to receive, to offset its time value or postponement cost, which *includes* anticipated future inflation as well as the pure value of possession.

Getting back to our deferred gratification issue, I would be willing to bet ($x, perhaps) that the *net present value* of all your deferred future consumption and resulting gratification will actually be greater than the value to you of any consumption derived from frittering your money away in the here and now—if you adhere to my approach. (I will use the term "approach" rather than "system" because it is more fundamental than a system. It is a philosophy, an orientation, a realization, an attitude, a way of life. "System" sounds too much like what the race track tout would give you.) So we are not expecting you to sacrifice anything, in reality. The main reason for this pleasant state of affairs is the principle of compound interest, basically, a phenomenon to be elaborated in a later chapter. Save enough and your future consumption will be so great that its present value will actually exceed that of any amount of alternative present consumption, in other words. Do what I say, and you come out ahead. But there is no need to trust me. Find out for yourself.

Dedication, Determination or Obsession?

By now it must be clear that saving money, i.e., controlling one's spending, has more than a little to do with getting rich my way, your way, the easy way. The preliminary description of the recommended methods that I've offered thus far must seem like fanaticism, obsession, or compulsion. "Sure you could save money if you're a fanatical, compulsive saver," would be a fair reaction to what I've thrown at you so far. And there would be an element of truth to it.

Yet the approach I am giving you is not a manifestation of obsessive-compulsive behavior in the literal, clinical sense of uncontrollable thoughts or impulses (luckily for anyone who chooses to adopt it). In fact, it is just the opposite. We are carefully selecting thoughts and perceptions, to develop preferences and tendencies, to bring about the ultimate in control. When you produce the apparent miracle of wealth without high prior income (_apparent_ to outsiders who do not know our simple secret, that is), that will be a monument to your supreme control. So our program for easy wealth-creation qualifies as "obsession" only in the colloquial sense of the word, in the most positive and salutary sense of single-minded determination or focus.

But how does one cultivate this determination, this self-discipline or dedication to purpose that makes such a seemingly unattainable money-accumulation tendency something relatively easy or second-nature? There are ways.

Self-Management Techniques

Perhaps you call it "self-control," "self-restraint," or "self-discipline." Regardless, the field of psychology has developed a well-grounded approach to managing one's own behavior—that is, inducing desired behaviors and preventing or extinguishing those that are not wanted. This is known as the science of *self-management* and it involves two primary methods: (1) *controlling one's environment* in such a way as to make the intended behavior more likely (or the non-intended activity less likely), and (2) imposing *rewards and punishments* on oneself in response to good and bad (desirable/undesirable) behavior, respectively.[3] In our case, the right behavior is saving money (so you get rich quickly) and the wrong behavior is needless spending, of course.

Environmental Control. What can you do to exert the right kind of control upon your environment? You probably have never even thought in those terms before, so it is high time you started. It is time for you to begin proactively shaping your *relevant* personal environment to make it easy for you to get rich without even making very much money. That task may turn out to be far easier than it sounds.

Recall that our essential purpose here is to increase the likelihood of you doing the kinds of things that will lead to your saving of money—and, in turn, getting rich fairly quickly. One simple, straightforward approach to environmental correction, therefore, is to *remove opportunities for indulging in the improper behavior*. Within our context, that means eliminate chances, as much as possible, to spend money. How can you do this? Some ways are perfectly obvious: Don't go to the mall—too many extra spending opportunities. Or at least don't spend as much time there. Be purposeful; buy only what you need and then *get out*. Or change your routine, if that routine presents too many spending temptations. Or change your *route*. Literally, you may wish to alter your daily transit route to or from home so you pass fewer stores. (But don't sacrifice efficiency, i.e., don't burn too much gas.) Avoid *people* who tend to lead you into money-spending situations. Or (contrary to the earlier suggestion) shop at less convenient, more crowded times, so the whole process takes longer! More *wasted* time, in a shopping environment, means less time for spending money. These offerings, admittedly, are prosaic, some even odd or extreme, but it gets better.

Take less cash with you when you go out. Or don't take your checkbook at all. If you fail to buy something as a result, you're ahead of the game. That just means you could do without it anyway, by definition. Or leave the credit cards at home. Some people have even resorted to the radical measure of destroying their credit cards altogether, cutting them into pieces and throwing them away, as you've probably heard and maybe considered.

Concerning credit cards, incidentally, one of the most basic principles of personal finance is to avoid their onerous interest rates, usually a "financing charge" of about 15-20%, by always paying the outstanding balance in full each month. Not to do so is completely irresponsible. If you don't already do that, you're crazy. If you don't do it, you don't have much of a chance. If you don't do that now, start immediately. That should be your *first* financial objective. (The second is building up emergency savings equal to six months' worth of income.) To actually *borrow* money to support current consumption, which is what you are doing by carrying credit card debt, is contrary to everything this book, as well as every responsible source in personal finance, stands for.

Try staying home more often, where conditions are less conducive to the spending of money (though modern communication technology, and even some old technology like the mail and telephone, certainly facilitates spending). Rent a movie or watch TV—or even read a good book or play monopoly!—instead of doing costlier forms of out-of-home entertainment. (Do as I say, not as I do, on this one only. I don't even own a VCR or DVR. Though my own historical proclivity was to go out several nights a week, as mentioned before, I've *already got money* because I generally have followed the same guidance I'm providing you in this book. In fact, I invented most of it. Besides, I hardly spend a discretionary dime on anything else.)

It may help to remind yourself how much money you are saving whenever you forgo expensive entertainment, so keep track of it. Even I have learned to moderate in recent years, using that device.

Or try alternative *outdoor* activities that don't cost money. How about a walk in the park or a day at the beach? Maybe you can think of other pleasurable recreational activities, outdoor or otherwise. After all, the best things in life are free, as they say.

You don't like these suggestions so far? A walk on the beach or in the park is too (forgive me) *pedestrian* for you? There's more.

Psychologists also recommend reducing environmental *cues* associated with the unwanted behavior.[4] In our anti-spending context, this could involve avoidance of magazine and newspaper ads, and store catalogs. Leave the room or divert your attention when the television commercials appear on the tube. No problem, you say? You're not influenced by advertising? You are, more than you realize, believe me. I'm in a position to know that.

I could go on, and you could go further. How about using a wallet or purse that is extremely cumbersome, inconvenient, and so dysfunctional that it makes it difficult and bothersome to remove money or credit cards? That's the spirit, isn't it? Or how about a wallet or billfold that is so unattractive, i.e., old and shoddy or ugly, that you are embarrassed to display it for use in spending?

You don't like any of these colorful ideas? Now that you have the environmental control perspective, you may be able to create some control devices of your own that you like better. If not, there is another aspect of environmental control that may be more appealing and productive.

Covert Conditioning. Recognizing the awesome power of the mind, psychologists tell us not to overlook the simple practice of just thinking about a problem in the right way. Various ways of thinking about something can direct the outcome of an issue in accordance with the thinker's desires. Right thinking can promote the right result. This method is sometimes known as "covert conditioning." Toward our financial end, there are several variations of this approach that I can recommend.

First, just maintaining generally positive thoughts about the favored behavior, while thinking unfavorably about the contrary behavior, may help attach the correct relative valuations to each, over time, at least subconsciously. Repeat after me: "Spending impoverishes, saving enriches. Saving my money makes me wealthy, and can give me financial independence. Spending my money keeps me poor, and dooms me to a future of failure and stifling mediocrity."

Visualize the stagnation, disappointment, and sorrow you will suffer throughout the rest of your life if you never have appreciably more financial resources than you have today. And what are your prospects for ever getting rich? Are you assured of ever *making* big money? Think about living hand-to-mouth into retirement, after which *real* hardship begins. On the other hand, feel free to fantasize and dwell upon a life of affluence and comfort, even substantial wealth, that can and should be yours if you abide by my programmatic instructions. Think of the vast spending and consumption possibilities available to you in the not-too-distant future, if you just give up the relatively trivial and piddling alternative expenditures in the present. Fantasize? Actually, it is not fantasy at all, as I and others have proven. Refer again to the tables of Chapter 2. Or go back to Table 1-1. Wouldn't you like to have a bankroll of *any* of those amounts, even the lesser ones? You can, and it shouldn't take very long.

Need more incentive? O.K., let's go all the way and put it right on the table. What would be the primary benefit to you of the achievement of real wealth? Be honest. Maybe there are some physical amenities or tangible goods or services that you have in mind. The inevitable increase in personal liberty that accrues from greater economic resources is also not to be dismissed. (Numerous people have given their lives for that concept, let alone its realization.) But for a very high proportion of humans, maybe a majority, attention naturally turns to the social realm. Do you suppose there might be some social or interpersonal benefits if you were to become rich? Do you think your social life might improve? Is it not conceivable that *better sex* would be one possible outcome of your financial success? Doesn't that tend to be true generally? Isn't that a very prevalent motive, along with power, for many people when it comes to money? Isn't sex a common underlying purpose of the pursuit of wealth, with good reason? As Aristotle Onassis once said, "All the money in the world would have no value if women did not exist."

Are there any "hot buttons" I haven't pushed yet? Excuse me if you think we've descended straight into the domain of the lurid, but let's get real. Go ahead and ponder or visualize all the benefits you think would accrue from wealth. Do so as much as you feel like. Psychologists do recommend such role-playing to internalize the right, and *useful*, kind of thinking.[5] Essentially, your correct understanding of the choices you face, and all their ramifications, will lead to the proper attitudes toward the alternatives, from which the most rational and optimal behavior will follow.

This "covert conditioning" approach may be viewed as a kind of mental self-coaching. Some other applications of it also may be of interest, and may help advance our common financial cause. In addition to the kind of *descriptive* thinking we've just covered, e.g., visualizing, fantasizing, and role playing, *prescriptive* thinking can help as well, maybe more. In other words, you can effectively issue commands or recommendations *to yourself* mentally. One proven technique is to tell yourself "Stop!" or "Don't!" when about to engage in the wrong kind of behavior, such as unnecessary spending.[6] And don't hesitate to sternly berate yourself when you think you deserve it, *à la* "Don't do it, you moron! Don't spend that money. If you do, it's just more of the same old rut and you'll never amount to anything, then you'll die in the gutter, where you belong—*if* you don't have sense enough to change your stupid behavior." (Did I say that?) Ridiculing your own current, counterproductive spending pattern can be effective. Give it a try. In fact, psychologists who specialize in this area advise spending about twenty minutes a day for several weeks on such self-coaching.[7] If a few weeks worth of twenty minutes a day can help ensure your future wealth, then that is time and effort well-spent, one of the few types of spending we approve of for you!

Again, the emphasis is on attaching positive or favorable thoughts to the desired behavior, saving, and negative or unfavorable thoughts and imagery to the non-desired behavior, which is unnecessary spending. If you're ready for a couple more illustrations, I have some good ones for you.

1. Every time you make a purchase, imagine tearing up or burning that amount of paper money. Dollar by dollar, or twenty dollar bill at a time, you see yourself destroying money equal to the purchase amount. That can be very painful. And it is an accurate representation because burning money is exactly what you are doing. Is spending still as much fun as it used to be?

2. Psychologists suggest associating *intensely disagreeable* imagery with the behavior you are trying to avoid, the more intense the better, to wit:[8] Visualize yourself making a purchase. See yourself going into a store, going up to the cashier, reaching for your wallet or purse, opening it, removing your cash, credit card, or checkbook, and making a purchase as you normally do. But this time, something is wrong. Just as you had entered the store, you began to feel ill. As you shop, inspecting merchandise or whatever shoppers do (I wouldn't know), the feeling gets worse. You are really sick, queasy in the stomach. By the time you arrive at the sales counter, you are dangerously nauseous, and you know you are in trouble. You are in a cold sweat, and bile is beginning to well up. Reaching for your money nearly brings it on, so you'd better hurry before you disgrace yourself. You wish you were home hugging the toilet.

Then, just as you begin to handle your money, you can't hold it in any more and you throw up all over the merchandise, the counter, the cash register, the sales clerk, and yourself. You are physically ill, really ill. Spending has made you sick. (Spending money *should* make you sick.) Vomit is all over the place, including you. It's all over your clothes, your hands, your chin. You're so embarrassed you wish you were dead. Then it gets worse. Your mess is so bad that it makes the cashier sick and she pukes all over you. This, naturally, makes you throw up some more. The cycle begins again. You can't leave because you are stuck to the floor! It is like a bad dream, but it's not. You're in hell.

And you *deserve* that kind of punishment. You deserve it for throwing your money away. You deserve to go to hell for depriving yourself of a future of wealth, for committing the sin of spending too much. The temporary and mild purgatory of self-controlled consumption spending, which will lead you to the promised land, is far preferable. *Not spending money* is much better than receiving a large dose of someone else's vomit in the face.

Repeat as directed, twenty minutes a day for several weeks. Force that mental imagery upon yourself every time you go shopping, or even think about going shopping. Once again, pardon me for taking this discussion straight into the sewer, but that is the appropriate place for the concept, or the reality, of impoverishing yourself through excessive spending when *the alternative is easily attainable*. That *is* financially sick, and sickening, so the imagery is fitting. If you don't like it, don't knock it until you've tried it. You need to develop an abhorrence of spending your money, and this psychological ploy may be worth a try.

Why do I impose this on you, aside from its aesthetics? Remember, the topic is unpleasant imagery and its psychological impact. Imagine that every time you buy something, you have to throw up. That is part of the purchase price, in effect. Considering how much you genuinely are damaging your future by spending money, the true price of most purchases probably *is* comparable to getting sick. Dwell on that for a few weeks, at least twenty minutes per day, as the doctor (that is I) prescribes. (But don't blame me for this technique. It comes from the respected field of psychology. And as the purpose was to come up with the most disgusting possible mental imagery to attach to the rejected behavior, I have to ask: How'd I do?)

2a. A variation of this approach is to recall the worst pain you've ever experienced—toothache, broken bone, whatever—and think of it every time the money-spending temptation surfaces. Again, you want your subconscious to associate the two, spending and pain, to make the first less desirable because of its psychological attachment to the second.

Self-Reward and Self-Punishment. Another well-established approach to self-management is based on what you do *after the fact* (as opposed to the kind of *prior* shaping of behavior we've been examining). You grant yourself rewards for the right behavior, and impose self-punishment for the wrong behavior. The most basic level of reward and punishment you can self-administer is, once again, what you *tell* yourself. Do not neglect to praise yourself for the desired behavior of not spending. Congratulate yourself, as you fully deserve to be congratulated, whenever you have resisted the destructive urge to spend money unless the spending is absolutely necessary. Feel free to acknowledge yourself as superior, a cut above the rest, when you take a step along the path to financial and personal freedom by *not spending your money*. And then, by all means, make a point of criticizing yourself severely if and when you deviate from the intended course. Castigate yourself any time you commit the act of abject idiocy by diverting yourself from the known and easy route to wealth and true liberation. Don't hold back. Don't spare yourself. A good portion of self-ridicule can be healthy, such as "You jackass. You had a chance to actually get rich, and now you are destroying that opportunity! That is absurd. That is financial lunacy."

But why is spending money so bad, you counter-argue? "I *enjoy* shopping and buying things. I *like* the things I buy. If they didn't give me pleasure or satisfaction, I wouldn't buy them in the first place. I am pleased to *have* the things I purchase," you may say. If you ever find yourself thinking this way, an appropriate response to yourself would be: "Typical consumer imbecile. You have missed the whole point. Are you not smart enough to grasp the point that your *net present value* from consumption may actually be greater if you defer your spending for awhile, until you have amassed your fortune? Would that not provide you even greater satisfaction?" If not, you may be a rare and hopeless case.

Do these methods seem trivial and insubstantial? Maybe they seem so but there is evidence that such self-reward/punishment can be effective in achieving self-control.[9] They can actually work.

Tangible rewards and punishments can also be employed. Like what? Anything that doesn't cost money, for starters. Any time you resist the temptation to spend money, indulge yourself in some way. Play a favorite music CD (one you already have; don't buy a new one). Watch a TV program you like. (If you don't own a television, don't buy one.) Sleep in an extra half hour. Take an extra-leisurely bath or shower, or just take an hour of time for yourself. Engage in some other activity you like best. (The best things in life are free, right?) *You* think of something. How should I know what appeals to you?

What do *I* do to reward myself? Nothing. I already do exactly what I want to be doing nearly all the time, virtually 24 hours a day, every day of my life. But I've already made it. So what *did* I do while I was in the process of building wealth? Again, nothing. The realization that all I needed to do was control spending, and that, in turn, would inevitably lead to financial security, was enough reward for me. I did not need to resort to the kind of supplementary rewards psychologists suggest. Maybe the correct realization alone will be enough for you, too.

Self-punishment is another matter. Examples of penalties you may impose on yourself whenever you commit the offense of spending money might include:

- Don't clean the house or apartment—until you can't stand it any more.
- Wear ugly or worn clothing. (Sackcloth, anyone?) Don't buy any new clothes, of course, *yet*.
- Use your least attractive in-home decorations.
- Don't wash the car for awhile.
- Stay home instead of going out partying.
- Be nice to someone you don't like (short of giving away money, of course).

- Terminate your cable TV subscription, or a favorate magazine subscription. (Obviously, some of these suggestions are money-savers in their own right.)
- Keep the price tags on merchandise, not only because it looks so tacky (punishment) but because it reminds you of how much money you've blown.
- Miss a meal. (Removal of a positive reinforcer can be as effective as applying something negative.)
- Abstain from some other enjoyable physical activity. (Maybe you can think of something that would be real penance.)

If you don't like these ideas, psychologists have some even more extreme offerings:

- Flick yourself with a rubber band until it hurts.[10] (Self-flagellation or whips and chains, anyone?)
- Punch yourself in the nose, or have someone else do it.
- Apply painful electric shocks! (Be careful—not to be tried at home without supervision! Again, don't blame me; these measures are from the psychologists.)

Once more, I never needed devices such as these, either. If you do benefit from self-administered reward or punishment, whether moderate or severe, psychologists make one additional suggestion: It should be applied *very soon* after the relevant object behavior for maximum re-inforcement, to establish a clear psychological association between the reward (or punishment) and the desired (or objectionable) conduct—in this case, not spending vs. spending.[11]

Self-Observation. All this one really means is record-keeping. At least for awhile, keep track of your spending, by category, as shown in the examples of Tables 2-5, 2-6, 2-8, and 2-10. All you need is paper and pencil.

How is this elementary bookkeeping supposed to help you get rich? Several ways: First, it is a form of *diagnostic evaluation*. Itemizing the application of your dollars, or finding out exactly where your money is going, enables you to identify opportunities for improvement, for cutting back on spending. When you realize the true magnitude of your spending in certain areas, perhaps for the first time, you probably will be surprised, possibly shocked, and the potential for low-effort cost reduction should become clarified. Relatedly, this specific knowledge also facilitates *goal-setting*. Once you are no longer ignorant of your categorical spending levels, you can establish targets. Aim for lower spending levels in various categories (which should be recognized as readily attainable when you finally have seen, through the record-keeping, how much you are wasting), especially those that will propel you fastest toward your saving and wealth-building objectives. Nothing complicated here—this is all just a basic part of the process. Goal-setting, of course, is an important step in goal-achievement. "A problem identified is a problem half-solved," or something like that.

Another corollary benefit of such "self-observation" (a fancy term for counting your dollars spent, in our context) is that it enables *projection* of the future. Rather than just a rear-view mirror look at what you have done, right or wrong, in your financial and consumption past, such a record is a basis for forecasting (a) how much you will have saved up, or how much you will be worth, at any given time in the future, and (b) how much time it will take to reach any particular desired amount of wealth. When making projections, just remember to take into account future return on your saved, and invested, dollars. In other words, if you save $5000 a year, does it take five years to save up $25,000? No, it would take only about three years and ten months, assuming an after-tax rate of return of 9% this time (which is realistic for a moderate-income person in the 28% tax bracket, also assuming a pre-tax return of 12.5%—typically available from the stock market in recent decades).

Two other benefits of financial record-keeping, again "self-observation" in the nomenclature of psychology, are not to be overlooked or underappreciated. First, it can be a financially-*therapeutic* habit. That is, the practice can actually influence your behavior in a positive way.[12] The establishment of goals relative to your current spending levels, or even the mere identification of your present spending pattern (or overall financial condition as in Tables 2-2 and 2-7), can serve as an incentive to change. Such records, even the crude ones I've shown you, can provoke you into being dissatisfied or disgusted with your existing financial conduct (even without contemplating puke). Negative attitudes toward one alternative thing (spending, not saving, not getting rich) will tend to prompt the opposite on your part, and then you're on your way.

The kind of record-keeping we recommend can also be a powerful incentive to show continuing improvement, to avoid backsliding, to make sure one year's level of spending or wealth is better than the prior year's. I know it worked that way with me; you can make a game or contest *with yourself* out of it, as I did. I made damned sure my net worth increased (from $17,679 to $17,787 to $18,796 between 1977 and 1979; Tables 2-7c to 2-7e) on a salary of $4000 and $6000, and with no tangible sacrifice! I chalked that one up as a win, for sure. I won that game on the way to winning the only championship I was after (other than earning a Ph.D.). I won that battle, and I feel as though I've won the war. If you had as much money as I report in Table 2-7(t-y), wouldn't you feel the same way?

Try this exercise. Try to remember all the useless, trivial, or frivolous purchases you made in the past year. Or, alternatively, do the review for as far back as you can remember. (For routine purchases, think back over the past month, then multiply by twelve for an annual estimate. For assistance in recalling big-ticket items bought, look around the house, and go through checkbook and credit card records. Don't forget *services*, as well as goods.) Make sure you include everything that you now consider a mistake to have purchased, decisions that seemed reasonable at the time but now can be recognized as errors. Then estimate, add up, the total of all those purchase prices, which would therefore be the total amount of money you've wasted on unnecessary spending just over that time period. How does that make you *feel*, as they say? Don't you wish you had that particular extra sum of money in your pocket, or in the bank, right now? Also recognize that if you had invested those dollars (and cents—let's never forget the cents) in even a conventional savings account or bank CD paying 4-5%, the present value to you would be substantially greater than the amount you've calculated.

This has been retrospective. Now let's look ahead prospectively. Suppose you stand to waste the same amount of money in the coming year (or whatever period you've just examined)—*or*, suppose you prevent that hemorrhage of cash. You *can*, therefore, have that extra amount of money—and more! You still have the power to stop its outflow.

So the next time you even consider buying something not absolutely necessary, something you may later recognize as a mistake and a waste, something that may cause you to laugh at your own foolishness, think again. That one act of thought, especially if done again and again, can make you rich.

Incidentally, on financial goal-setting, I admit I have set some specific numerical targets in the past, namely: $50,000-100,000 in net worth by age 35 (after having practically nothing, relatively, as a 30-year-old student), a quarter million by 40, half a "mill" by 45, and a million dollars by 50. I believe establishing such goals may actually have had a slight beneficial effect on my pace of accumulation. (I have met all the goals so far either literally or approximately; I went over the quarter million dollar mark *while* I was 40, not *by* 40. Close enough.) However, incremental goals such as year-to-year or monthly improvement in financial leakage, i.e., spending (as opposed to aggregate wealth-oriented targets), should be much more motivating because of their immediacy, I feel. But the other kind of longer-term, macro targets may very well work better for you. So why not try them all?

Finally, self-observation via financial records can truly qualify as a *punishment*. As you can imagine, keeping track of spending categories, *à la* Tables 2-5, 2-6, 2-8, and 2-10, is a real pain in the ass. (Records of net worth, as in Table 2-7, are much more interesting to compile.) Observation of your senseless spending behavior may be painful in and of itself. That's good. The observation, or written recording, of your financial profligacy can deter its continuation, as already mentioned. But you can also use the disagreeability and nuisance of record-keeping as a contingent motivation. In other words, make a deal with yourself. Promise yourself that you will only undertake this clerical chore until you achieve one or more financial milestones, such as getting your spending down to a certain level or raising your saving or wealth up to a certain level. Then reward yourself by terminating the onerous duty, or at least reducing your record-keeping activity. That is the kind of thing I did to energize myself to get this book finished. I promised myself I would only keep exact track of certain things (such as some of the tables you've seen and others to follow) until completing this project. That prospect of relief was a strong motivator for me, and you can do the same type of thing to control your own undesirable tendencies, like spending too much money.

Can simple practices, including mental tricks and devices such as the ones described in prior sections, really succeed in making you rich? "Get serious," you say. Seriously, indeed, some very good psychologists verify the effectiveness of those techniques. Even the record-keeping part is important. Self-observation is considered a crucial preliminary step in self-regulation,[13] and some of the preceding material demonstrates why. You may not think you have the potential or capability to achieve such behavioral change, to get yourself to do something so different, but you may surprise yourself. The *individual* is actually the one in the best position to manage his or her own behavior, because the individual is the one closest to the behavior and with the best access to it, according to psychologists who work in this field.[14] Give it a try. What do you have to lose? You're already losing tons of money.

And please note, above all, none of this involves *willpower*. The self-management techniques I've reported do not rely on willpower to change your financial and consumption activity (and results), but rather involve purposeful, yet straightforward, *manipulation* of your situation or environment to accomplish the desired results. Review the methods to see that they are the kinds of things anyone could do. (O.K., so maybe a modicum of willpower would be needed for some aspects of the approach, like the self-punishments or forcing yourself to keep records. That is hardly an intolerable burden considering the ultimate reward.)

No, it certainly does not require superhuman willpower. All you really have to do is put the "system" in place, apply the methods, and then let it happen. Then you are on automatic pilot to become rich, fairly quickly and very easily, and *without making very much money*. That is how I did it. As I've stated, the only environmental manipulation I really needed was the idea, or the realization that it truly is possible to do what

I've told you can be done. Given that, I knew exactly how the future would play out. I knew that I would soon get rich without making very much money, and I just enjoyed sitting back and watching it happen, effortlessly (as shown in the illustration). You can do pretty much the same. So what are you waiting for?

If you wish to learn more about self-management beyond the general outline and illustrative examples I have provided of this highly useful set of techniques, I recommend the following book: *Self-Management: The Science and Art of Helping Yourself*, by Brian T. Yates (Wadsworth Publishing Company, 1985). The volume is a very practical, step-by-step manual or "cookbook" approach to regulating your own behavior. It should be helpful to you if you need any help, if you need more than the foundational idea I've given you. The idea alone may be enough, as it was for me. If you don't like the guidance from the field of psychology that we've just gone over, I have some of my own to offer that you might like better—coming right up.

Chapter 4

Other Ways to "Psych" Yourself into Getting It Done

What is the most important thing in the world? What value or principle is the most important to you personally, the one thing you cherish most of all? Different people will answer in different ways, of course, but for a large segment of the population in the Western world the supreme value would have to be *freedom*. So important is individual freedom or liberty that it is prized more than life itself by many. Proof of this is the large numbers who have given their lives in freedom's service and pursuit, as mentioned before and as witnessed in the formation of the United States of America and many other nations.

What in the world does all this have to do with your getting rich? It is a potential motivator. Freedom, or the possibility of attaining a higher level of it for yourself, is one major reason for you to adhere to the program of wealth accumulation embodied within this book. Inevitably and obviously, more money means greater economic freedom which translates into more personal liberty. The more money you have, the broader the range of choices you have available, and that is the very definition of freedom.

A major part of this economic and personal freedom, of course, is *time*. The more money you have, the more time at your disposal—because of the less time you must apply to your economic needs. Or think in terms of how long you have to work to be able to buy various necessities or other products. How long must you work to earn enough money, after taxes, to buy a house, a car, a suit, a pair of shoes, or a good meal? That is what you are discarding by spending money when you don't have to. You are throwing away and wasting part of your life, your most precious possession, each time you spend money. Time is money, but money is also time.

So keep all of this in mind if you need any additional motivation to enact the simple things we have seen it takes to get rich without having to make very much money. The correct perspective, the main thing to keep in mind, as you embark upon our simple and easy plan to become wealthy is that you are actually *buying your freedom.* By not spending money you are literally purchasing a lifetime of tremendous freedom. Every time you forgo a purchase, each time you do *not* buy something, you are making a down payment on a future of prosperity and greatly enhanced liberty. Perhaps realizing this elementary reality will make things easier for you. Maybe this understanding will help energize you to perform the tasks necessary to *get rich without making very much money,* though those tasks are simple enough as it is. (And I hope this bit of personal philosophy is received better by you than it was by a girl friend of mine a few years ago. After I made the mistake of candidly sharing this philosophical-financial perspective one evening, the next time I saw her she sarcastically greeted me with, "Hi. How's your freedom?" That's O.K. You'll get rich and she won't. The last I heard she was still looking for a rich doctor to marry.)

Do you need more? All right, then, do it for your country.

What? How does saving money by you and me benefit our country? Because it would improve the national saving rate, and the United States economy desperately needs a higher saving rate. Compared to about 15% of income the Japanese save, and a saving rate of over 8% in the U.S. a few decades ago, net national saving has fallen to 1% of gross domestic product (about 3% of disposable personal income) for the United States. So what? Some very detrimental consequences, that's what:

Low *savings* means insufficient *investment* or *capital formation*. (Those who remember Econ 101 will recall that saving translates directly into investment.) Deficient investment means insufficient capital available per worker throughout the economy, and that causes the problem of *lower productivity*. This, in turn, means *lower wage income* per worker, higher *prices* (i.e., more inflation), *higher interest rates* (because of the greater need for firms and government to borrow required investment funds), more *foreign capital inflows* (because of inadequate domestic capital), a *poorer balance of trade*, more *income flowing out* of our country (because foreigners own a higher proportion of national debt), possible *recession*, and higher *unemployment*.

Bad things result from insufficient saving by you and me. Good things follow from a healthy amount of national savings—things like investment in productive capital, low inflation, higher worker income, a favorable trade balance, a stronger dollar—and that is what makes the world go 'round, or at least keeps our economy healthy. We could easily extend this analysis by pointing out the devastating *social* effects of a bad economy, including crime, broken families, poor education, drug addiction, and despair, or the negative impact on the natural *environment* of excessive spending, consumption, and waste.

But isn't consumer *spending* what's good for the economy? Isn't that what you've always heard? Well, don't worry yourself about the amount of spending, economy-wide. Sure, aggregate spending drives the economy, but we've got plenty of spending. What we as a national economy need to achieve is a *slight* alteration of the proportion of saving to spending. If the saving rate is 3%, that means the spending rate is 97%. If we can nudge saving up to 8%, for instance, that would constitute only about a 5.2% *relative* decrease in spending, but would represent a *167%* increase in saving. The economy would be a lot healthier that way, and if all readers of this book do exactly as the book recommends, I'm sure that will produce just the right modification of national saving! Now go and do your part. We're on a mission from God.

Or is this still not the right motivator for you? If economic patriotism doesn't move you, then let's try *fear*. Think about whether you will have enough money for retirement, and how reliable government programs like Social Security are likely to be. Then "be afraid. Be very afraid." (We could probably highlight *every* point with a famous movie line if we tried hard enough.)

The scary truth is that few people today are saving enough to provide for even a minimally comfortable retirement. Someone earning $100,000 now will need $653,000 of savings (in today's dollars) by age 65 to retire at the same standard of living. (At least $350,000 is needed for the average income worker.) Yet the average person saves only 31% of what will be needed; savings rates must *triple* for prospective retirees to keep up.[1]

Only 3% of American retirees are financially independent. A study by Merrill Lynch, the prominent brokerage house, reveals that the average middle-aged American has only $2600 of net financial assets. Twenty percent of Americans have saved *nothing* for retirement; another 13% have saved between $1000 and $9000. Annual savings in 401(k) retirement plans average $2400, with total account values averaging only about $33,000—among those who even have these accounts. Average *total* savings across all American working households is only $18,750![2]

Many in the "baby boom" generation, now approaching 65, have been especially reckless financially to the point of jeopardizing their retirement. *The Wall Street Journal* reports that the typical customer of a credit counseling service "is 38 years old, earns $38,000 a year . . . and has 11 credit cards and almost $20,000 in credit card debt alone."[3]
All this is a crisis. It is an out-of-control situation. It is crazy. This is a ticking time-bomb not only for individuals and families, but for a generation and the nation.

Compounding the crisis, maybe *your* crisis, is a constellation of related facts: People are living longer. Medical costs are rising, as is the cost of living in general. Nursing homes cost over $60,000 a year now.[4] How much will they cost when *you* are ready for one? There is a trend toward earlier retirement. Social security and pensions combined will only cover 20-40% of your retirement income needs.[5] Given all this, you may very well face the unpleasant dilemma of living in elderly destitution or having to work past normal retirement years. (This concern is especially critical for women, as they live longer than men.) Factor in the reality of corporate downsizing and layoffs, and you may have a much more immediate need for some substantial savings. Again, what are you waiting for?

And there is an urgent need for you not to wait. If you do, you will miss out on the tremendous power of *compounding*. If you save only $2000 per year in an IRA for *ten* years beginning at age 35, earning a 10% return (a reasonable, conservative expectation of what you can get from the stock market, based on its history) *and add no more*, the nest egg would be worth $230,000 at age 65. However, save and invest $2000 a year the same way for *twenty* years beginning at 45, and you only have $126,000 by the age of 65. If you invest $2000 annually in an IRA for *eight* years at 10%, starting at age 20, you will have $855,503 by age 65![6]

Or go ahead and continue to spend your money, and then die in the gutter. See if I care. See if anybody cares.

Not provoked enough by foreseeing the down-side? Then don't forget to enjoy the up-side. I have already implied, more or less, that adhering to our program for getting rich without making very much money can actually be fun. I would guess the satisfaction one can derive from such a pursuit, and achievement, is self-evident. As one astute financial author testifies, "It feels good to save money. Emotionally, it's what we need."[7] But there is more. Think of it: Getting rich *without making very much money*, and you are clever enough to do it! You actually have the capability to do such a thing. (Even now you are rapidly developing that capability.) You are one of the chosen few now— though almost everyone has the same *potential* ability. Think of it as a game, a contest that you are winning hands down. The thrill of victory, etc.! Think of it as beating the system, which you certainly are doing, and that is always a satisfying feat. Apply that mentality to the task and you may find special enjoyment. You can now sit back, comfortably, and laugh at all the rest, the losers. Do what we have outlined, as I and others have done, and you will not only be achieving and living the "American dream," you will be *conquering* the American dream. You will be turning the American dream inside-out and on its head. You will be putting your own special stamp and "spin" on the so-called American dream. You will be doing it differently, the easy way, a novel way, an unheard-of way, a way other people, *ordinary* run-of-the-mill people, cannot even imagine. You're good enough, you're smart enough . . . . You get the idea.

Do you still need more reasons to do what it takes, minimal as that is, to get rich the easy way? O.K., I'll give you 36 of them. I recently came across some attractive philosophy by a financial guru named Richard C. Young, a self-made millionaire. He declares that "Wealth flows most freely to those who desire it." You've just got to want it badly enough, in other words. Anyway, to *help* you want it badly enough, if you don't already, Mr. Young lays out "The 36 Greatest Joys of Wealth," or "What Would You Most Enjoy about Being Wealthy?" Here they are, to assist the motivationally-challenged,[8] with no elaboration from me:

- I am set for life. I never have to worry about money for as long as I live. What a wonderful way to go through life!
- I have purchased the most precious commodity I have on this earth—my time. I relish the freedom to spend it any way I see fit, giving more to my family, my favorite hobby or outside interest, whatever.
- I can look forward to retirement without anxiety because I have more money and a higher income than I'll ever need.
- I can laugh at inflation. Since I'm always growing richer, I'll always stay ahead of it.
- I can kick the dust off my shoes and spend as much time as I like traveling this wide world, stopping at all the cities I've always dreamed of visiting—Paris, London, Rome, Vienna, Madrid, Venice.

- I never have to worry about the financial impact of a major injury or illness . . . or long-term nursing care, for myself or any family member.
- I can accumulate massive holdings in stocks, bonds, real estate, gems, gold, etc.
- I possess the knowledge to generate plenty of money from my investments under all conditions. I delight in the awareness that for as long as I live, I am always growing richer.
- I can afford to send my children or grandchildren to the best schools and give them the best possible head starts in their young lives.
- I will never be forced to be financially dependent on anyone, and this gives me a great feeling of self-sufficiency.
- I have permanently eliminated all financial stress from my life, and it feels so good.
- I can live in a bigger house, even a mansion if I so desire.
- I own a cottage by the sea, or perhaps a cabin on the lake in the mountains. It's my own little hideaway to which I escape for delightfully refreshing trips whenever the spirit moves me.
- I can help my loved ones live out their dreams.
- I can start the new business I've always wanted and not even worry if it fails. (It's a lot more fun that way.)
- I can indulge my passion for the car or boat of my dreams. (I can see myself riding in it right now.)
- I can hire my own butler, live-in housekeeper or cook who knows how to whip up my favorite dishes just the way I like, whenever I want.
- I can collect and display in my home magnificent examples of fine art, antiques, oriental rugs and other stunning collectibles.
- I can entertain lavishly and be known as the grandest host in my social circle.
- I can own a celebrity's wardrobe of the finest custom-made clothes, shoes, and accessories.

- I can vacation in the most fabulous and scenic vacation resorts in the world—Tahiti, the Riviera, Caribbean, etc.
- I can become a highly influential contributor to my favorite causes and be a voice that is heeded. My influence can make a difference to our world.
- I feel more secure than I ever have in my life. Better yet, I know this Gibraltar-like security will never leave me, and this inner security has a marvelously uplifting effect on my whole personality.
- I don't have to work at any job I don't like. I can take as much time off as I like and go anywhere I please, without asking any one's permission.
- I can afford the best health care for my family.
- I can live anywhere in the world I want. Hawaii . . . Bermuda . . . Cancun . . . or all three!
- I have the freedom to dine out and shop without regard to price as often as I wish.
- I can give the most generous gifts and support to anyone I care about—my children, parents, favorite charities, etc.
- I can leave a very large estate and be gratefully remembered by my heirs for making their lives easier and more prosperous.
- I am regarded as extremely successful by my family, friends and acquaintances. (If my friends from high school could only see me now!)
- I do not have to take orders from anyone. And while I may love my work, I relish the luxury of being able to say to any boss who becomes belligerent, "thanks, but no thanks" . . . and walk away any time I want. (I don't need any job because I derive all the income I'll ever require from my investments.)
- I relish the peace of mind I enjoy from being 100% debt-free.
- I can have fun by pretending on occasion that I'm Silas Marner and, when no one else is home, sneak into my bedroom and run my fingers through heaping leather sacks of gold coins, antique

silver dollars and rare gems. Just owning these riches gives me undeniable pleasure.

- But I'm not just a "closet Silas Marner." I'm also a "closet Santa Claus" who enjoys nothing more than to surprise people with generous, even outlandish, gifts when they least expect it. I especially love to do this with children.

- I can lavish upon the love of my life the most luxurious gifts in appreciation for years of devotion—a jeweled necklace, a diamond ring, a ruby brooch, a red Corvette convertible, or tickets for a year-long cruise around the world on the *Queen Elizabeth II* (first class, of course).

- I absolutely love the power and freedom of being able to do what I like, when I like, with the people I like. I am not beholden to anyone, and will hold my head proudly until the day I die, knowing I will always be financially self-sufficient. In the meantime, I can buy what I want without hesitation. I live life on my terms, no one else's, and that's the way it's going to be for me from now on.

- All of the above.

There you have it, count 'em, from millionaire Richard Young, and that ought to be enough. If none of those "36" grab you, then maybe you can think of something that *would* appeal to you personally about being rich. If not, if you still can't summon an adequately mobilizing attitude, there is still hope for you. The answer in that case is *just do it*, to coin a phrase. Just start saving money.

Seriously, if you are still having difficulty inculcating the right attitude, the attitude that will inexorably lead you toward getting rich easily, an alternative starting point is with your own *actions*. There is a tendency in human nature for attitude to follow from behavior, sometimes. So if you start acting a certain way (controlling your wasteful spending, in this context), the desired attitudes are more likely to occur naturally, in a way that is consistent with your behavior. In turn, the attitudes then produce and reinforce the correct behavior. In other words, just start to reduce your spending a little bit, observe the positive results as you begin to accumulate some savings, and discover how that feels, what a kick it will be for you. The feeling will probably make you want to experience more of it, and that is the idea; that's the drill.

Are we introducing will-power into the formula after all? Only a trace. It shouldn't require much effort to not spend money on one occasion, and then another, and that is all we are asking. That is the beginning. "A journey of a thousand miles begins with a single step." Or just spend *less* on a few occasions. According to professional consultants who specialize in changing human behavior, "individuals can alter their approach to financial issues by making *incremental* changes [emphasis added]. For example, rent an economy car rather than a luxury model on your next vacation; shop for less-expensive brands at the grocery store; buy clothes or other goods at off-season sales."[9]

So "just do it," or more accurately, *just don't do it.* Since our profoundly and remarkably simple program to easily achieve the seemingly impossible doesn't really require you to do anything, but instead involves *not* doing something, the watchword is "just don't do it." Can you do it, or rather *not* do it? How hard can it be? Try it. All we need is a slight adjustment in your behavior and then it snowballs, with the rest falling into place very automatically. And remember, this *behavior first* strategy is a fall-back position for those who can't find the right natural motivation among the dozens that have just been offered. At least something from among those motivators should resonate with most people, though, I would think.

Or *can* you do it? Perhaps you are still thinking that you just can't save money, no matter how hard you try, even if you are motivated to do so. There goes that destructive, inhibiting, conventional perspective again, similar to what we saw at the beginning of Chapter 1. Don't think the way the rest of the world thinks! Most of those people are losers anyway, at least financially, based on published statistics reporting how pathetically little savings most people have. You are a cut above those others, aren't you? *Now* you are, for sure, by virtue of your willingness to see things differently—as verified by reading this far into a book that offers you a different way.

Can't save money? Don't make me laugh. I and others, probably many others, know better because we've done it, and we've done it easily. I showed you how I not only lived on $4000-6000 a year, but I actually put some money away! You can become a millionaire making about minimum wage ($20,000 a year), as has been documented. As we've also seen, you can become a millionaire on savings of $2.74 a day ($1000 per year). You can't handle that? Sure you can. Or save half that and have half a million.

Again, don't take my word for it. The authors of an off-beat financial self-help book titled *Your Money Or Your Life*, Vicki Robin and Joe Dominguez of Seattle, have demonstrated that they can live on $6000 per year, far below the official poverty level, and have done so for over twenty years.[10] They insist they have not sacrificed life-style. (More on the kind of specific practical advice to be gained from that form of experience will be presented in Chapter 6.) A former IBM employee and now a reformed yuppie, Diane Grosch of San Francisco, lives on $6,500 a year—but has more free time than ever before and is financially independent! "I used to spend $200-300 a month on dinners out. Now I buy in bulk and pay attention to sale ads," she says.[11]

If you still doubt your capabilities to accomplish something that isn't very difficult, in fact doesn't even require you to actually *do* anything, please bear with me a little further. Maybe I can persuade you that I am right, that you certainly can achieve it, that you actually can *get rich without making very much money.* You see, I fundamentally believe that nearly any human, if channeling his or her talents in one direction only, can achieve superior, or at least competent, performance. That is a roundabout and roughly equivalent expression to the familiar, "You can accomplish anything if you set your mind to it." The focal task at issue in this book is so simple, despite superficial appearances, that it should be no problem for nearly anyone to accomplish to a superior degree. You should have little or no difficulty in doing a first-rate job of getting rich without making very much money. Unquestionably, we've all observed people succeeding at much more difficult tasks, haven't we? Considering how easy it is to get rich without making very much money, I'll bet *you* have done more difficult things successfully at one time or another. Think of the most difficult task you have ever accomplished. Rather than my asking you to do *that* again, aren't you glad I'm only challenging you to enact the idea in the title of this book? Doesn't that seem easier by comparison?

Speaking of *comparatively easy*, try the following "top ten" list.

TOP TEN THINGS THAT ARE *WAY* MORE DIFFICULT TO DO THAN WHAT THIS BOOK PREACHES

10. Hold Michael Jordan (or LeBron James) to fewer than 20 points.
9. Hold Michael Jackson to fewer than 20 boys.
8. Watch the Chicago Cubs play in the World Series.
7. Celebrate Hanukkah with Mahmoud Ahmadinejad.
6. Invite Hillary Clinton and Monica Lewinsky to the same party.
5. Diagram any sentence uttered by George W. Bush.
4. Say "pardon me" to Bill Clinton and not get shaken down for money.
3. Get the truth out of Saddam Hussein (even when he was alive).
2. Get the truth out of Bill Clinton.
1. Be married to O. J. Simpson.

Though this list is as serious as a Letterman "top ten," each item in it is true, i.e., is truly more difficult than the program I've given you. The next list is more serious.

TOP DOZEN THINGS THAT ARE *REALLY* MORE DIFFICULT TO DO THAN WHAT THIS BOOK PREACHES

12. Get up in the morning.
11. Shave.
10. Select your day's attire.
9. Tie your shoes.

8. Eat breakfast.

7. Go to work.

6. Pour a cup of coffee.

5. Chew gum.

4. Have lunch.

3. Work out.

2. Fix dinner.

1. Choose what to watch on TV.

Every one of these dozen items is, in a true sense, more difficult than getting rich without making very much money, because every one involves some action or effort. Our program for wealth building requires less of you than things you routinely do every day. Is that easy enough for you?

Even more seriously, we have one more list:

TOP TWELVE THINGS THAT ARE *INCOMPARABLY* MORE DIFFICULT TO DO THAN WHAT THIS BOOK PREACHES

12. Learn to walk.

11. Learn to read.

10. Learn to ride a bicycle.

9. Learn to do arithmetic.

8. Graduate from high school.

7. Do the work necessary to finish any year of elementary or high school, for that matter.

6. Learn to play a musical instrument.

5. Learn to play a sport reasonably well.

4. Learn a foreign language.

3. Lose weight.

2. Have a good marriage.

1. Raise a child.

Each and every one of this last series of entries truly requires infinitely more enduring effort than getting rich without making very much money, which requires none. Yet millions or even billions of people have mastered each task, in some cases, obviously, a majority of all humans. They can't all be more able than you, can they? Enough said.

True Grit From Real Life

On the topic of people doing things that are much more difficult than what I am urging you to do, and trying to show you how to do, I have some true stories that will illustrate and, I hope, inspire. You may be familiar with one of them already.

You have probably heard the story of *Rudy*, from the Hollywood movie of the same name. Rudy (real name, Dan Ruettiger) was the kid from Joliet, Illinois who somehow got into the University of Notre Dame despite an undistinguished high school academic record and after tours of duty in the service and in the steel mill. Not only that, but Rudy then tried out for the Notre Dame football team, made the team as a reserve "scrub" player, and ultimately was allowed to suit up for a game, actually got into the game, made a tackle on the final play of the game, and was carried off the field on the shoulders of his appreciative teammates who respected Rudy's perseverance and effort. If you have ever doubted the veracity of this story, I can testify that it is true. I was there and I knew many of the people involved, including the title character himself. My parish priest even reported the episode in his Sunday sermon the following week, as the story of Rudy was already becoming renowned locally at that time, 1975, almost twenty years before Hollywood got ahold of it. That later aspect is the real phenomenon of Rudy.

Getting to play in a college football game is one thing. Getting a movie studio to produce a feature film about your life is quite another. I recall the first time I saw Rudy—the person, not the movie—after he returned to South Bend after having been away for several years. It was the late 1980s, probably '87 or '88. I happened to run into him on the Notre Dame campus whereupon he told me about his plan, or scheme, to sell his life story and have a movie made about it. Initially I thought, "Sure, kid," but as he told me more about the endeavor over the coming months and years, I began to realize he was serious, and mightily determined. He told me of his persistent efforts to get his screenplay accepted, or even read, by the author and producer of the famed movie *Hoosiers*. He even had me call *Hoosiers* producer David Anspaugh (ostensibly to put in a good word for him, for whatever that would have been worth), who ultimately did produce and direct the *Rudy* movie. When Mr. Anspaugh told me he was favorable toward the project, though it was no done deal at that time, I realized that Rudy's idea was something much more substantial than a quixotic pipe-dream. As Rudy himself would tell you, he got his story published through sheer persistence, by being a major "pain in the ass" to writers, directors, and producers until they finally capitulated to his cajoling. Rudy's story is a great one, an inspirational account of the indomitable human spirit and will. Alternatively, it can be seen as testimonial to how far you can get by being a pest and a nuisance, by not taking no for an answer—again, as my friend Rudy himself would tell you. They really should make a movie about how Rudy got the movie about himself made!

Now suppose my charge to you were: (1) Get into an expensive, prestigious, private university, even if you have little or no academic talent; (2) make the football team and make the final tackle of the season, even if you have little or no athletic talent; and then (3) coax Hollywood into making a movie of your life, even though you have no discernable talent for doing this. Would it seem like I was asking the impossible, or at least the highly improbable? Would such a mission seem even more implausible than what I *am* asking of you? Our simple program of saving money and becoming wealthy, fairly quickly and with little real effort, doesn't seem so extraordinary in comparison, does it? It's nothing compared to what Rudy did, frankly. So if you ever need more inspiration to adhere to the course of financial independence the easy way (and it is so easy that you probably *won't* need it), just remember: RU-DY! RU-DY!

To paraphrase Senator Lloyd Bentsen in the 1988 vice presidential debate with Dan Quayle, "I knew Rudy Ruettiger. Rudy was a friend of mine. You're no Rudy." But that's O.K. You don't need to be a Rudy. Your task is infinitely easier than what Rudy set out to do, and did.

Another account of improbable success, against all odds, comes from my own experience. When I was a senior in college, I was prepared to do almost anything to avoid the military draft, yet I had no conceivable way out after my student deferment was to expire. I didn't want to go to Canada (too patriotic), I didn't want to shoot my little toe off (too chicken, I don't like pain), and I never would have been able to convince my draft board that I was a conscientious objector (too poor a liar, or too honest, I like to think). I had a very low draft number, 92, and my pre-draft physical was scheduled at the Chicago induction center, notorious as the toughest in the country, i.e., they would take almost anybody. What was I to do? (If these considerations seem obscure to younger readers who have not had to face the prospect of involuntary conscription, ask your elders what it was like. Women may ask any man middle-aged or older.)

Then I came across a nugget of information that proved to be one of the most important finds of my life. It occurred not entirely by accident, because I was actively searching for draft-avoidance strategic information everywhere, and every way, possible—but it certainly was fortuitous in part. One evening as my time as a free civilian was growing short, a friend of mine, actually a former girlfriend again, just happened to mention that she knew of someone who had beaten the draft by having braces put on his teeth. Hallelujah! My prayers had been answered. That was my lucky day indeed. I knew instantly that I had found my ticket to freedom. (Good thing I've remained on good terms with most of my ex-girlfriends.) The story gets better.

I then approached my childhood orthodontist in Gary, Indiana, who had put braces on my teeth twice before when I was in grade school and high school. (My teeth never turned out quite right because I didn't have the fortitude to wear my retainer diligently. Good thing, again.) I told the doctor I wanted to undergo the treatment once more to finish the job right and, oh by the way, another motive is to become unqualified for the military draft. (It is true that orthodontic appliances are a disqualifier for military service on grounds that they are a condition requiring constant medical attention. At least that was true when I needed it to be true in 1971.) Fortunately for me, the orthodontist was sympathetic and agreed to provide the necessary certification and prolong the treatment as long as would be medically ethical. That turned out to be long enough to get me out of the draft permanently, to secure a "1-Y" deferment until my category was no longer being called up.

Don't get me wrong. My anti-draft motivation was based on pure self-interest, not leftist ideology. I'm as nationalistic and patriotic as the next guy, more so than most, if you hadn't guessed. And it was not a matter of fear of being killed in Vietnam, natural an incentive as that would be, because at the time in question draftees were no longer being sent to Vietnam. So no one was sent into that meat grinder in my place due to my skill, or luck, at draft-avoidance. (Bill Clinton is a draft *evader*; I consider myself a draft *avoider* through legitimate means.) I simply realized that two years of military service would have been an unproductive waste of time for me, personally (and for the military), especially compared to the alternative of a full-tuition scholarship to graduate business school, which I also had in hand. Can you really argue with my choice? But the story gets better.

The orthodontist did the job *for free*, regarding it as a job not completed that my parents had already paid for years earlier. Thank you again, doctor, Mom, and Dad. But the story gets better.

The downside I anticipated from wearing braces as a collegiate senior at age 22 was that they would be unsightly, and would reduce my effectiveness in the area of social activity, so to speak (not that I ever had that much success to begin with). I shrewdly decided to go forward with treatment on my *lower* teeth only, therefore, so the ugly silver appliances were of very limited visibility and did not seem to be a deterrent. To this day I believe I actually had better success with women during that braces-wearing period because the tooth-wear was such a novel conversation piece!

Getting back to our business, suppose I gave you this "mission impossible": You have a low draft number, you are only a few months from induction, you have no foreseeable way out of getting drafted, but you have to find one. Not only that, you have to do it for free and in a way that causes you little or no inconvenience. Now would that assignment seem more or less difficult than the one we have been discussing, the one embodied in the title of this book? Rightfully, the mission I am offering you is child's play by comparison. You're lucky I'm not challenging you to do something really difficult, like the following impossible mission.

When I was a college senior I did have one other serious matter on my mind besides beating the draft. I realized it was time to start thinking about what I wanted to do with my life, as I urge my own students to do currently. So I asked myself the question, "What is really important to you?" reflecting my understanding that it would be most rewarding to devote one's life to something really cared about. In answering, I realized that I was (and remain) supremely devoted to three entities: my parents, my country, and my school, the University of Notre Dame. (Perhaps you have heard that that particular institution tends to evoke intense loyalty among its graduates.) In pondering practical career paths derived from my designated values, I narrowed it down to (a) become President of the United States and somehow engineer the destruction of the Soviet Empire, or (b) dedicate my life in some way to my beloved alma mater. Trying to remain in or near the realm of the sensible, I picked *b*—a good choice since someone else with a Notre Dame connection, sort of (The Gipper), took care of *a*. Given my choice and objective, the next decision became: What form should my service to Notre Dame take? Of that, I was not sure.

To make a long story short (for a change), I am not the type who always wanted to be a university professor. But ever since I first heard that there was such a thing as a Ph.D. degree, when my college-educated mother explained it to me as a child, I knew I would have to give it a try some day. So the convergence of that long-standing underlying interest and the more contemporaneous selection of aim *b* above moved me to enroll in a doctoral program at a leading business school (the University of Wisconsin) a few years later, after I had gotten my MBA and done a few other lesser things. When I did so, naturally it was with the intention of someday returning to Notre Dame and joining the faculty as a business professor.

I won't bore you with this one much longer but it does become germane. You may be aware that the Ph.D., or Doctor of Philosophy, is one graduate degree they don't exactly hand out for coupons, S & H Green Stamps, or bus tokens. Aside from coursework, written and oral comprehensive exams, and completion of an original research project called a dissertation, the doctorate is a *knowledge*-based degree like no other. For example, the essential responsibility of a student preparing for the comprehensive exams is *everything that is known by the field in the subject area*. Then, for those who have the endurance to complete the degree, usually taking from three to five years beyond the master's, there is a competitive job market. Ph.D.'s entering the academic job market will typically interview with a dozen or more universities in the hope of getting at least one offer. (That part of the process is not unlike most job search situations.) When I was finishing my Ph.D., I interviewed with only one school, Notre Dame. My teachers and fellow students at Wisconsin thought I was crazy, and may very well have been right. I just told them all, "If I don't get hired at Notre Dame, I'll just go tend bar somewhere." (No, I didn't mean that literally. I would have pursued other options eventually. Even as a nose-to-the-grindstone doctoral student, I still had a sense of humor.)

Beyond all this, there were about 80 other applicants for the one position I was seeking. Of the four or five of us who survived several screenings and visited for on-campus interviews (comparable to the plant visit interview in the commercial recruitment context), I am certain that I was far from the favorite. Unlike the others, I had attended the school as a student, so the people making the hiring decision *remembered* me, unfortunately for me, as a less than serious character. I had that additional obstacle to overcome. Somehow, apparently through the grace of God (Notre Dame might express it differently) or some cosmic accident, it happened for me and I joined the Notre Dame faculty, as intended, in 1980. Then, in 1988, I was granted tenure. Believe me, that part of it was not easy either. When my friends say I've hardly worked a day in my life, it only looks that way from the outside.

The moral of this story, once again, is: Suppose I gave you the assignment that I undertook. Pick *one* university in the country. Then go get a Ph.D. degree, get yourself hired at that one particular school despite overwhelming odds, and then publish enough scientific research to get tenure. What would be the probability of succeeding at any phase of the sequence, let alone all of them in conjunction? The assignment you are about to undertake—if you choose to accept it—is far easier and much more probable, isn't it? Or would you rather go start work on a Ph.D.? Get real, and get going. Get started getting rich. (If you do want to earn a Ph.D. despite what I've described, you have my admiration. It won't prevent you from getting rich easily, as I've also shown.)

Is this reported episode a contradiction to our "easy wealth" theme? No. Note the distinction: Getting rich is easy because almost any job should do it for you. For me to get this one particular job is what was hard.

But enough about me, probably too much. One of my old buddies from college (nicknamed "Nasty John" for reasons we won't get into), retired at age 39, but he consciously set the process in motion to lead to that result *when he was in his early 20's*. I know, because I was there. I remember the day he told me of his plans. We were shooting pool in our favorite bar, Corby's, back in South Bend for a football weekend just a couple of years out of school—we couldn't have been more than 25 years old at the most. My friend John was in his second or third regular job, working in sales or finance for a Cleveland toy company. He told me, in between pool shots and beers, "You know, if this job works out for me the way I think it will, I could really cash in big. Those stock options could be worth a few hundred thousand dollars in a few years." Fifteen years or so later, after John had worked his way up to vice president, those stock options turned out to be worth many times his expectations when the firm sold out, and he retired a multi-million-aire (yes, at age 39. I can show you the clipping from *The Wall Street Journal* announcing his retirement.) I believe John has been having a very good time ever since.

Obviously, the preceding saga is not an account of getting rich without making very much money. John made a lot of money. But his story is one of achieving an objective, a seemingly long-shot, implausibly high-aspiration, objective, that most people would think unrealistic and therefore not even attempt. But John made it, as a result of *one decision* at *one moment in time* (in a seedy bar, no less), and in a relatively *short period of time.* (What were you doing 15 years ago? Was that so long ago? Don't you wish you had started saving money 15 years ago? The future is *now*, as football coach George Allen said.) The future course I am proposing for you is a lot easier to enact than what my friend John chose, and did, isn't it? Suppose you had delved into this book and then discovered that the "secret" scheme was to become a corporate vice president and then make millions on stock options years later in a buy-out deal. Forget it, right? What a hoax! Everybody can't do that. Most people are not in a position to do anything like that, you would balk.

Correct. But instead of that long-shot scenario, which in fact is per-fectly plausible as my friend proved, I offer you something much easier and far *more* realistic. Before you reject the simple route to riches that I lay out for you, be grateful that I did not waste your time with an ap-parently extreme, off-the-wall plan like my friend John pursued—suc-cessfully, of course, in his case. Presenting you with a John-like vision, though demonstrated to be possible, would not have been legitimate because I also promise *easy*, and what John did would not be easy for ev-eryone. What I am giving you should be easy for almost anyone. So stop whining and get started. What is your financial future if you *don't?*

Or take the case of my parents. In approximately 1970, on low in-come, only five years away from retirement, and while supporting a kid in college and one or two country club memberships, my parents had almost nothing saved. Yet within a few years, they amassed the kind of wealth shown in Tables 2-2(a) to 2-2(m). If you are beginning to realize, and are ready to accept, that it is possible to achieve success financially, that it is easy to get rich (as many others have demonstrated), then I will now spare you. I will stop belaboring the principle, but only if you promise that you have accepted that it can be done, and that you can do it.

If not, if the motivations and illustrations we have just reviewed do not resonate with you, then I give up—almost. Think of "The Little Engine That Could." Think of the song "High Hopes." Think of Rudy or *Rocky* or *Forrest Gump*. Or don't think of anything. Just get started. Just do it.

Is that all there is (to coin a phrase, again)? Is that all there is to it? Is *austerity* all I am recommending as the secret to getting rich? Is it just a matter of becoming a miser, for crying out loud? Become a tightwad, be stingy, niggardly, or penurious, and you've got it made. Is that the message? Repeat after me: "Greed is good." Is that it? The unambiguous answer is no, and yes.

The primary underlying qualification for being able to get rich without making very much money is the capacity to identify what is really important to you. Is getting wealthy important to you? Is a level of financial independence and security previously unimaginable to you something that you would desire? Of course it is. Is buying all those things you "want" important to you also? Is unfettered consumption of goods and services of importance to you? Sure it is, but how important? Is it more important than the gaining of true financial independence—in the near future, no less? Is frivolous spending really more important to you than putting together a nest egg that qualifies as substantial wealth? Surely not. (If it still is after all the coaching I've just given you, then it might not be productive for you to read further. You might as well put the book down, walk right out the door—if you're not on a bus or airplane—and start looking for diamonds in the street. That's as much of a chance as you have. On the other hand, you will be receiving some practical guidance on the *tactics* of saving money, as opposed to the philosophy, in the next chapter, so you might want to hang in for awhile.) *Of course* an element of frugality, thrift, or tightwaddishness is involved in the recommended process of getting rich without making a lot of money. How could it be otherwise? But the main point to understand and appreciate is, if you can identify what is truly important to you, it is no longer like being a miserly tightwad. It doesn't seem that way and it doesn't *feel* that way, because it all comes naturally and automatically at that point. That is why our procedure for getting rich does not involve any discernible sacrifice. Once you no longer want the usual objects of your spending *as much as you want the alternative*, getting rich, then not spending your money is no longer unattractive to you.

So greed is good, after all? No, and yes. We are not talking about greed. "Greed" is a pejorative term, an ugly appellation for an entirely wholesome human tendency, a nearly universal drive. There is nothing wrong with a desire for financial security. There is nothing wrong with attending to your own economic self-interest. That is nothing less than human nature. There is nothing improper about trying to provide for the welfare of yourself and your family. Ambition is not crass or immoral. Rational self-interest is not unsavory. Don't let anyone tell you otherwise—while you're getting rich without making very much money, or after you've done it.

Don't forget, either, that our national economy depends on concentrations of wealth. Private concentrations of financial resources are necessary for the successful functioning of the U.S. (or any nation's) economy because it is those pools of funds that serve as sources of investment capital. That capital, in turn, then leads to all the economic benefits enumerated earlier—for you, me, and everyone, i.e., productivity, jobs, stable prices, etc. (It is not *poor* people who provide jobs for other people.) When you start putting together your own concentration of wealth, you will be doing your part for your country, therefore.

It is in that sense that "greed," actually normal self-interest, is good. So you may feel free to feel good about it, and anyone who doesn't like it might as well get used to it. In fact, you should celebrate this healthy and benign reality, if you're not too busy getting rich.

So all it takes, essentially, is the right attitude? That's all there is to it? Yes, and yes. Some recently published research has reported that the #1 distinguishing characteristic of American millionaires is their *attitude*. It just so happens that the millionaires' attitude is the same as I have described, exhorted, and tried to transmit to you in the preceding pages. According to the study, the hallmark of the rich person's attitude is the tendency to *live below one's means*:

> The most successful accumulators of wealth spend far less than they can afford on houses, cars, vacations, and entertainment. Why? Because these things offer little or no return. The wealthy would rather put their money into investments.... It's an attitude.
>
> As many millionaires see it, a luxury house is a bad investment. Why pay $500,000 when a $150,000 house will do? That extra $350,000 could be earning interest or building equity.... The person who piles up net worth fastest tends to put every dollar he can into investments, not consumption. All the while, he's reinvesting his earnings from investments and watching his net worth soar.[12]

A very high proportion of American millionaires (about 80%) are self-made, first-generation wealthy. Typically they live in middle-class neighborhoods, drive plain old cars, are compulsive savers and investors, and live by certain financial rules, such as:

- Focus on wealth, not income. Income doesn't matter very much! (See, what did I tell you?) Riches are determined by what you accumulate, not what you spend or earn.

- Wealth is the inescapable outcome of perseverance and self-discipline. (As we've also seen, if you internalize the correct attitude, it doesn't even require very much conscious self-discipline.)
- Develop a goal, such as a certain dollar figure of savings or net worth by a certain time limit. (It is always reassuring to learn that we have followed the millionaires' formula, isn't it?) Then dedicate yourself single-mindedly to that goal.[13] (Do it the right way, of course, and it doesn't even involve any real effort. It is all a matter of what you *don't* do.)

Then the millionaires' attitude toward money tends to be manifested in some revealing and colorful ways, like these:

- A New York financial research firm has found that the richest segment of the U.S. population is among the "chintziest." According to the firm's spokesperson, "Among all the people we invite to participate in focus groups, only the extremely wealthy—those with liquid assets over $1 million—ask if they can take home the extra sandwiches and cookies."[14]
- Sam Walton, the Wal-Mart billionaire, drove a pick-up truck until his dying day.
- Warren Buffett, currently the second richest man in America, still lives in the same house in Omaha he bought for $32,000 decades ago. He also cares nothing about clothes (a man after my own heart in that respect, too).[15]

If you needed any corroboration, if you didn't believe me, I hope this empirically-based testimony suffices. As the author of the cited study, a management consultant and former university professor, says, "Attitude is the greatest difference between millionaires and the rest of us.... If you make wealth—not just income—your goal, the luxury house you've been dreaming about won't seem so alluring. You'll have the attitude."[16] In fact, as I suspect you've realized by now, attitude *no longer* is the difference between millionaires and us. We are now of them, in that regard. We have come to share the attitude that is the key to great wealth. (If you *haven't* internalized the attitude, I suggest you either stop reading or reread.)

Chapter 5

Practical Principles and Tactics: Some Details on *How* to Make It Happen

So where are we? You are at point *A* and you want to get to point *R*, for *rich*. (Maybe *A* stands for *abject* poverty, then, or possibly *average*.) The route that has been laid out for you is surprisingly direct and hazard-free. First comes *awareness* or initial knowledge of a lightly-traveled and smooth path through the financial wilderness. Other tourists apparently haven't discovered this way, and it's yours for the taking.

Then comes *understanding* or the full realization of the opportunity that has been handed you. No, it is not a mirage. It's really there—a straight line or a smooth trip to wealth. Take it. Don't look a gift horse in the mouth, as it were (another expression your author just made up for the occasion).

But you are not going by horseback. It is more like stepping onto an automatic people-mover, ski-tow, or electric tram that takes you all the way to where you want to go automatically. It certainly is not a high-speed bullet train. You *could* take one—there is a parallel route upon which lies its track—but the fare would require more money than you have. Given the certainty, safety, automation, and effortlessness of the people-mover or tram that will get you to your destination fast enough anyway, you are more than satisfied with that mode of transport. (It is far easier, in fact, than driving your own vehicle, which would at least involve some real effort on your part. And you probably don't even own a car because you can't afford one, metaphorically.) The special benefit of this particular transportation form is that it is a convenient no-brainer.

You are indeed so satisfied with the prospect of this easy journey to your financial objective, when you didn't even know the way until very recently, that you have developed a very positive *attitude* toward embarking on the trip. It is that attitude that moves you to get started, to hop on the transporter and stay on. Once you do, your success is assured; it is automatic. In other words, the correct attitude has induced the proper *behavior* which, in turn, makes ultimate arrival at your destination (financial success) inevitable.

The most vital of all wealth-generating tactics truly is derived from the philosophical immersion of the last chapters. Once you realize getting rich without making very much money is really possible, and simple, a favorable attitude toward pursuing that course should naturally follow. And if that attitude is enough to get you started (as it should be), to prompt you to try it, there is no reason for the intended outcome not to occur. As we saw in the first two chapters, it is elementary arithmetic: Income (I) *less* expenses (E) = retained surplus or profit. Any full-time employed person's I is great enough, and almost anyone should be able to keep E low enough.

The basic sequence that underlies the virtual inevitability of what otherwise would seem to be a financial miracle, therefore, is *awareness* ➡ *understanding* ➡ *attitude* ➡ *behavior* ➡ *reinforcement*, just as I and so many other marketing professors have diagrammed on the blackboard for our students in other contexts. I didn't make this up, although I may have invented application to the task of getting rich without making very much money.

Financial success *should* now be inevitable for you (though some might still be unsure about how to suppress the E component—we'll get to that), but we don't want to leave anything to chance. Therefore, we will be examining some very practical tactics that relate directly to the nuts-and-bolts of the process of getting rich without making very much money. We will be spoon-feeding you some pragmatic advice that should lubricate the engine that drives you toward wealth the easy way. (No more metaphors, mixed or otherwise, I promise—except a few.)

First, to reiterate, there is some *tactical* relevance (that means things you actually do, or concrete actions) contained in our philosophy of getting rich. You need a new way of thinking and, by George (and Abe and Alexander and Andrew and Ulysses and Ben), you have now been given a new way of thinking. Spending money unnecessarily has been identified as the enemy. You must oppose this enemy and, fortunately, all that's required of you is *passive* resistance. Think *not spending*—morning, noon, and night. When you get up in the morning, try to come up with new and creative ways to avoid spending money (short of stealing groceries from the supermarket or welshing on bills, I mean). Ask yourself, "What can I do to *not* spend money today?" In the evening, take a few minutes to review the day's expenditures and what you could have done to eliminate some and minimize others. Did throwing your money away on that junk really make you happy—as happy as getting rich? You only bought necessities? Sure you did. If so, I'll bet you could have spent less.

You must come to abhor spending and enjoy not spending. Reflect upon all those reasons for getting rich, those benefits listed in Chapter 4, and the fact that they are really possible for you to have. Then remember how spending your money in the present is what prevents you from having all those things you really want. Are you content being just like everybody else? Wouldn't you rather be a contrarian? Spending is your enemy, your opponent, and that opponent must be crushed. Death to spending!

Don't forget to try some of those psychological tricks we went over in Chapter 3. You should recall some of them vividly. They were designed to be vivid for maximum impact, to provide maximum deterrent to your unnecessary spending. Think puke.

In all seriousness, the way you *think* about money is a critical wealth-building tactic for you because it sets the process in motion properly and puts you on the right track. Getting off to a good start (on the way to making yourself rich without even having to earn a high income) is practicality number one.

Major Tactical Directions
To Budget or Not to Budget

You would probably guess that *budgeting* is another basic tool of spending control, saving, and wealth-creation for those who don't have the luxury of high income. No! Forget budgeting. The whole orientation of budgeting is wrong for our purpose. Budgeting has it backwards. Budgeting is concerned with setting *maximum* spending amounts for a given period. We don't even want to hear about maximum spending. Sure the intention of a budget is establishment of reasonable spending levels, but we go beyond that. We can do better than that. All you have to do is spend as little as you can get away with, minimize your spending or at least approach that goal as best you can, and you don't ever have to think about a budget or what the level of spending is relative to it. O.K., set the budget at *zero* for all spending categories and try to come as close as you can. That kind of budget is passable. Or exempt one or two categories, realistically (since you're human), and then don't ever spend an unnecessary dime, or cent, on any other. That's the right spirit, at least. I obviously have exempted a couple of recreation-related categories (e.g., Tables 2-5 and 2-10).

Instead of a budget, all you need is the kind of monthly expenditure records shown in Tables 2-5, 2-6, 2-8, and 2-10. Once you discover, through these simple instruments, where your money is going, opportunities for spending reductions will become apparent—especially if you also do the daily review (at least for awhile or occasionally) mentioned above. Such expense tracking should generate *instant savings of up to 20%*, according to a report in *The Wall Street Journal*.[1] This, along with some goal-setting perhaps, is the only financial planning you'll need—so don't ever pay a financial planner. We've just done that job for you, in effect, for only the price of this book.

What if you do this record-keeping and you *can't* identify potential savings? Try again and I'll bet you can. What if you still can't? Then your spending is at rock-bottom level and you are probably beginning to save money, initiating the process of getting rich sooner than you think. What if your spending is already at rock-bottom and you're *not* able to save money? You're probably wrong, about one of the two. What if you're *not* wrong? I'll answer that soon.

Life-Cycle Decisions: Married with Children?

You've probably heard the expression, "Two can live as cheaply as one." I don't think it could be literally true, but there surely are *economies of scale* deriving from marital union of two formerly independent economic entities. Examples of the available scale economies (which essentially means some common expenses spread across two people instead of one) would be one house or dwelling unit for two people, i.e., only 1/2 home per person needed whereas one per person needed before; some household utility expenses for a two-person household would be less than double those for singles, e.g., telephone, electricity. While I certainly would not recommend making such fundamental life choices based upon projections of kilowatt hours or mortgage payments, the happy conclusion is that marital status (single vs. married) is not necessarily a prohibitive factor in any way when it comes to pursuit of our financial aims. One obvious complication of marriage, of course, is that two people instead of one have to buy into any given financial regimen, such as ours.

The double income of two working spouses is not a scale-economic factor *per se* because the per-person earnings are just the average of the two. However, two incomes in a household may induce saving if a particular realization is also provoked. When my parents began their phenomenal surge of saving, of necessity as they approached retirement, the tactical constraint they imposed on themselves was to *live off one income, the lower of the two, and bank the other one*. That part wasn't so easy for them to do, at first, since the lower income was a

Catholic elementary schoolteacher's *very* low salary, but they did it. Thus illustrates the tactical implication of the dual-earner household: Dedicate at least one partner's entire compensation to saving, if possible. If my parents could do it, it should be possible for almost anyone.

Not to dwell on it, but my parents' insightful understanding and attitudes were the cornerstone of their success in getting rich quickly without making very much money. As I and others have already advocated in the preceding chapters, it is all a matter of attitude (and understanding is a large component of attitude). As one who came through the Great Depression and worked in a steel mill all his life, my father, naturally, has always known the value of a dollar. I believe he also shares my appreciation of the entertainment value of the *game* of getting rich without making very much money—i.e., the "beating the system" or contrarian aspect of it. When you enjoy what you are doing, you are able to do it better, isn't that right? It's attitude!

My mother traditionally had been one who believed "money is the root of all evil." After years of counter-propaganda from my father and me, she softened her attitude to "*love* of money is the root of all evil." Experiencing the wholesome, beneficial, and enjoyable progression depicted through Tables 2-2 and 2-3, she may have come around even more. After all, there is good money and bad money, depending on its purpose.

My mother's contributions to the admirable numbers of Tables 2-2 and 2-3 were largely the kind that are less visible overtly, but assuredly show up on the bottom line. I got my "never throw anything out" attitude from her, and I am grateful for it. (She has made exceptions for my old polyester, admittedly.) My mother was always mending, sewing, fixing, reusing, improvising, and all that, as well as cooking, cleaning, and earning. She made many of our clothes and other useful things. I can't even begin to adequately itemize or acknowledge. Of course, her economic contributions to our little family, substantial as they are, are surpassed by her spiritual ones. I only hope the dedication at the beginning of this volume transmits a sense of the true magnitude of tribute my parents deserve. Yet I fear it is not enough to signify my appreciation for *their* dedication to their only son; nothing I say here could possibly be adequate. (By all rights, that son should have turned out better.)

To head off any unfair misimpression I may have erroneously created, my parents certainly were not, and are not, *venal* in any way. Wealth-gain the way we have done it, and the way you can do it, is primarily a matter of attitude all right, but venality, "greed," or avarice was no part of my parents' formula. My parents can be described, in our economic context, as frugal, responsible, prudent, conservative, traditional, dedicated, and honest—it sounds like the Boy Scout creed and signals, correctly, that *virtue* is highly compatible with financial success—and those conventional words are grossly insufficient to describe those two fine people who have done so much for me. I won't begin to try here. I won't begin to try to thank them for being so understanding when their teen-aged son smashed up the family car (an Invicta convertible, but a conservative and traditional one) three times within about a year. (When friends of mine meet my folks for the first time, they invariably are amazed at how *normal* my parents are.) Forgive the emotional digression, but it is not out of line in view of the significance of the topic and achievement described.

I recently asked my mother what her secret formula was. If not a formula, what had been her approach to such successful frugality? Could she at least report some of the highlights or ingredients to us? In response, she wrote this:

Our first furniture was "hand-me-downs" which we painted and I slip-covered. Dad made a bookcase of bricks and painted boards. Later, when we moved to Ambridge (a section of Gary), he made a hutch for the dining room from a dresser.

You slept in (cousin) David's bed. You later wore some of his clothes. I'm still wearing one of his jackets you had worn (forty-five years earlier). (Dad's sister) Wanda and (her husband) Eddie gave us a floor lamp, later a set of dishes. (Sister-in-law) Dorothy and (Dad's brother) Harry loaned us a dining room table and chairs.

When we moved to Miller (another section of Gary) in 1946, we had no stove and no refrigerator. It was almost impossible to buy either during the war. Dorothy loaned us a hot plate and I used a window sill for food. Fortunately, it was cold out. Due to the finagling of friends, we eventually got both pieces.

I made my own clothes. In 1945 I needed a winter coat for work. I ripped apart an old coat of Dad's, used an old blanket for interlining, and quilted it to new lining. I wore that coat for several years.

Plan menu from what's on sale. Now save with coupons.

When I wasn't working, I dressed my hair myself. Maybe that's why I let it grow: didn't have to pay to get it cut. When I was a child, I never had much money for clothes, but my mother (that would be the author's grandmother who died before he was born) told me I didn't need a lot of clothes if everything was ready to wear. Hang up clothes not being worn. Keep them clean, pressed, and mended.

Dad: Always change clothes and hang them up. Keep shoes repaired and polished. Soap: saves slivers on new bar. Cuts own hair.

Pick up pennies. Save uncancelled stamps.

Plan meals to be divided: cook once and serve twice. Cut up the chicken yourself. Make your own stew meat. Use toaster oven for small amounts.

Soap: Let soap dry, put on sponge or brush. Unwrap scented soap and put in lingerie drawer awhile before using it.

Shopping: Scan ads before making out list.

Shoes: Rotate shoes. Put in shoe-trees between wearings. Buy good shoes that fit and they will last and look nice and be comfortable.

Labor: Unless you would otherwise be gainfully employed, your labor is free—making clothes, washing your car, preparing food from scratch. Biggest expense to any item is someone else's labor.

Laundry: There is a water-saver attachment to my washer. Used soapy water is retained in a stationary tub. This I use to wash small rugs and cleaning cloths, or to scrub floors or toilets, before putting it down the drain.

A gift from my own mother to you, this was. Accept and adopt the attitude that shines through, and you will prosper.

Ironically, just within the past few days, as of this writing, my mother has worn a couple of different sweaters that had been mine in my junior high school years, over 45 years previous. That's beautiful. The payoff certainly is beautiful, as seen in the measured results of Tables 2-1, 2-2, and 2-3. Again, for the record, that payoff was a comfortable middle- to upper-middle-class living standard on very low income in the early years, and then rapid wealth accumulation in the later years.

The tactical relevance of attitude cannot be overemphasized. To capture the salutary attitude my mother brought to our family's legitimate pursuit of economic self-interest, I close this segment with an old New England proverb that sums it all up. My mother, who got it from her mother, gave it to me to give to you.

Use it up.

Wear it out.

Make do,

or do without.

You wouldn't want to argue with my mother, would you?

From the sublime to the ridiculous, or from the sublime to the slime, on the subject of marriage and money: What about divorce? The financial implications are well-known. It can be very costly to one party (aside from non-monetary costs), possibly both, or one party can gain. It is less than a zero-sum game, though, because of legal expenses and the loss of scale economies. You can go to the library and find literature on the economics of marriage and divorce.

Once again, strategic life-cycle choices probably should not be made just to conform to financial exigencies (the issue is tactics, not strategy), but one, or two, should certainly be cognizant of the financial ramifications of such major decisions and the accompanying changes in life status. As one who is happily single, I am the last to be lecturing anyone on these matters, but I can call attention to objective reality: About 50% of all marriages end in divorce. Of those who remain married, what proportion are miserable? Get married and there are long odds against you. Attitude may be of supreme importance if you want to get rich, but knowledge or understanding underlies attitude. Having an accurate understanding of the true odds pertaining to your alternatives could turn out to be worth big money to you.

As so many married friends have told me, "I love my wife, but you did the right thing, John." As I tell them, "A woman would have to be crazy to want to marry me, and I'm not about to marry a crazy person, so it's a 'Catch-22.' I'm safe." This concludes the presentation of my general philosophy of marriage. I will now stop commenting on something I know absolutely nothing about.

From the ridiculous to the sublime: What about having children? What is their financial impact, especially on the opportunity to get rich without making very much money? Is it still possible with children?

According to some recent estimates by the U.S. Department of Agriculture and *American Demographics* magazine, the average child costs about $6000 in total expenses just in its first year of life. Some of these costs include disposable diapers (about $600), food and feeding equipment ($900), furniture ($1000), clothing ($400), bedding and bath supplies ($250), medical and personal care products ($400). A very conservative estimate of total child-rearing cost through the age of 18, for only one child, is $100,000.[2]

What does this mean for your wealth accumulation if you are a parent? Does this eliminate your chances? Maybe not, but it doesn't make things any easier. Take a look at Table 5-1, which first repeats the wealth-building projections of Table 1-1. Assume those amounts in the first column of money numbers are what you could save up if you had no children (at annual savings of $5000 or $10,000, over time horizons of 5/10/20 years respectively. We'll dispense with the 40-year forecast for brevity.) The next column presents the cost of child-rearing, for

TABLE 5-1

IMPACT OF CHILD-RAISING EXPENSE ON SAVING POTENTIAL

	From Table 1-1[a]	Expense per Child[b]	With 1 Child	With 2 Children
$5000 annual savings @ 8%:				
5 yrs.	$ 31,680	$ 34,148	$ -2,468	$ -36,616
10 yrs.	78,227	79,199	-972	-80,171
20 yrs.	247,114	229,478	17,636	-211,842
$10,000 annual savings @ 8%:				
5 yrs.	$ 63,359	$ 34,148	$ 29,211	$ -4,937
10 yrs.	156,455	79,199	77,256	-1,943
20 yrs.	494,228	229,478	264,750	35,272

[a] Operationally assumes no children, i.e., if this column represents your total childless savings or wealth, last two columns adjust for one and two children, respectively.

[b] $6000 first year expense + $4,947/yr. over next 17 years = $100,000 total; @ 8%.

---

one child, based on those cited estimates of $6000 for the first year, $100,000 over 18 years. (Remember, this money also earns a negative return, in effect, by preventing you from earning the assumed 8% on these dollars. That is also taken into account in the listed numbers.) As you can see in the subsequent columns, "baby" really takes a big bite out of your bankroll. At $5000 in annual (childless) saving, one kid wipes you out, actually putting you in the hole for the first ten years at least (subtracting the second column from the first). With an annual saving rate of $10,000, one child cuts your wealth roughly in half over all three time frames. Two children? Forget it; you're buried. (See last column which subtracts double the expense column from the initial column.) Then there is the added cost of putting offspring through college, which this analysis does not even address.

So is the lesson from this that you cannot have children, at least more than one child, and still get rich without making very much money? Not quite—there is still hope.

• Note that the initial savings projections *assume* $5000 or $10,000 per year. Higher saving rates are certainly possible. You have recently received evidence that *much* higher rates are attainable, even on very low or moderate income. Don't rule out the possibility that you could achieve a base rate higher than those shown, thereby allowing you the option of one big happy family (featuring a child or two or more) *and* wealth.

• Remember one of our fundamental rules: You have to make a choice. Another possibility, therefore, is to choose children instead of other luxuries, such as going out partying all the time. If I can do what I did financially, doing what I traditionally did recreationally, you can achieve financial security while attending to more elevated and responsible pursuits.

• Realistically, and obviously, you should limit your reproductive output to one or two offspring to support—if you intend to get rich the easy way. (This discussion does not even entertain the immoral alternative of *not* supporting your children. I'm sorry I brought it up.) If you have more than two children, you *can* still get rich, but you will probably need to make some money. Our program and methods are directed at those who need to get rich *without* making very much money.

• If you violate our basic financial prescription by having multiple children *and* not making very much money, you can *probably* forget about getting rich any time soon. (Not necessarily, though; a counter-example appears in Chapter 9. There is still a chance, but you will have to sacrifice much more than our plan specifies.) You may indeed be happier that way. It depends on what is important to you. However, if you do abide by all the other principles you find in this book, you inevitably will be *better off* financially than you otherwise would be. The attitude you receive from this book's teaching will still serve you well, and make you a little richer in money as you make yourself richer in family. That is the best consolation prize I can offer, but it is ultimately your choice.

Twenty-two percent of U.S. families earning between $25,000 and $100,000 per year *claimed*, in a classic 1994 poll, that they could not save *anything* the preceding 12 months, and another 46% whined, I mean claimed, that they only saved 4% or less of their income. Evidence from a 2007 study shows that most American families have saved up *nothing*.[3] Now, as promised, an answer to those who claim, or whine, that they just *can't* save: I believe these people can be classified into three categories.

(1) Those who really *haven't tried it*. Until you have given a fair test to those attitude and behavior change devices of Chapter 3, including some of the psychological gimmicks, you have no license to complain. And you haven't even seen most of the more down-to-earth saving suggestions to be elaborated in this and the next chapter. If you, right now, are still doubting the viability of what I have laid out for you, then you probably do not yet have the right attitude, the "wealth building with ease"-assuring attitude. We will try to correct that.

(2) Those with a *self-imposed constraint*, such as violation of the proscription against having an excessive number of children (and then still expecting to be able to get rich *without* making very much money). Another example would be long-term unemployment. As acknowledged, even by me in my irresponsible youth, you probably have to have a full-time job of some kind (at least for awhile), even at minimum wage, to enact our program of getting rich without making very much money. Let's be reasonable.

(3) Those who *really can't*. I will concede that there may be some with extreme or unusual circumstances, such as uninsured medical expenses, involuntary unemployment, or other financial emergencies, who genuinely cannot conserve their money. I firmly believe, with some basis, that those with a legitimate excuse for an inability to save money are a miniscule segment of the population. After all, if I can increase my wealth on a $4000 salary…! Even these people, though, should be in a *better off* position financially if they try to adhere to our wealth-building principles, so this book still should be valuable to all in its target audience, which includes all who do not make a lot of money.

One reaction you may have at this point, or may have had earlier, is: "Sure, prof, it must be easy to save money if you never have to buy an automobile or clothing. I could save money, too, if I got all my cars and clothes for free!" Fair enough. So let's just subtract or erase the financial equivalent of the cars and clothing your author has received as gifts. That's seven cars—all used, remember—over the past 35 years: maybe about $50,000 worth plus interest, surely less than a hundred grand, though probably close to it. (Sorry I don't have the energy to estimate this answer more exactly. How much could that '65 Belvidere have been worth, anyway?) Throw in the value of the clothing I *would have purchased anyway*, which wouldn't have been much, and can we agree that $125,000 (in net present value) is a rough monetary estimate of the special largesse I have received from my family? Subtract that number from the most recent total of Table 2-7, and my corrected net worth would be 91% of its current gross value. Would you be pleased to have that proportion of any of the bottom lines of Table 2-7? Would you throw away any of those amounts?

Never having had to purchase an automobile or clothing in my entire life is meaningful to me on several levels, certainly, both pragmatic and sentimental. The primary appeal for me is the beautiful sentiment that such a beneficence embodies on the part of those close to me. Clearly, though, a 9% adjustment to a wealth-creation record is not disqualifying, does not indict the claims I have made, and does not undermine my case example—especially since any decrement would be virtually offset by a corresponding *increase* in my parents' wealth. In other words, most of the savings I experienced from family generosity comes at my parents' expense, by definition. The correct perspective is that my parents' saving record is actually better than it looks in the tables, and mine marginally less impressive, but the total of the two is invariate for practical purposes (overall, it's a "wash"), as is the lesson those numbers teach.

"Can't save"? No excuses, please.

A Basic Principle of Personal Finance: The Miracle of Compounding

You may be familiar with some of those cutesy examples of the power of *compound interest*, such as:

(1) If, on that first Christmas Day about 2000 years ago, Saint Joseph had invested *one dollar* in a savings account earning only *1% interest*, the account balance today would be over $425 million.[4]

(2) Which would you rather have, $1000 a day for 35 days or a penny *doubled* every day for 35 days? The first option leaves you with $35,000, of course. Starting with a penny and then doubling the amount you receive each day puts you ahead on the 22nd day, at $41,943.04. Your total is $1,342,177.28 after 27 days. At the end of the 35 days, the happy total has become $343,597,383.60![5]

(3) During the Revolutionary War a group of British soldiers borrowed firewood from a colonial church, agreeing to incur a debt of $18 (translated into contemporary U.S. currency) at 6%, but then neglected to pay up. Some 183 years later, in 1961, the church officials presented the British government with a claim for about $750,000 based, appropriately, on compound interest. Had simple interest been the basis, the claim would have been for $216.[6]

No less than Albert Einstein is reported to have said that compound interest is the most powerful force on earth, and he knew something about powerful forces.

That power is readily illustrated by a comparison with "simple interest." If an amount (say $1 or $1,000,000) is invested at simple interest of 4% per annum (year), i.e., if the 4% earned on the investment (4 cents or $40,000, respectively) is paid to the investor each year and held but not reinvested, it will take 25 years for the original amount to double (to $2 or $2,000,000). At 4% *compounded* annually, with the same interest rate earned on all interest payments—which is the definition of compound interest—the original sum doubles in less than 18 years. Compounding, therefore, just means the earning of interest on interest. It represents a kind of accelerating "snowballing" effect, earning and growing at an ever-increasing rate.[7] (You can use the so-called "Rule of 72" to estimate how long it takes for an amount of money to double at any given compound interest rate. Just divide 72 by the rate, and the result is the number of years. For example, at an interest rate of

8%, the time for an investment to double in value would be about nine years.) If compounding is done more often than annually (monthly or daily at most financial institutions), then your money grows just that much faster.

Compounding means each of your invested dollars gives birth to off-spring, lots of "baby" dollars. Those baby dollars then grow up fast and reproduce themselves, in turn, and the cycle continues. It is from this lit-eral "generation" of compounding dollars, which produces accelerating wealth gain for an investor, that a couple of corollary principles emerge.

(1) *Don't touch your capital.* Don't ever spend your investment capital, i.e., money set aside for investment or that which is already invested. Doing so not only robs you of those dollars, but of a much larger amount made up of offspring dollars in the future. The farther you look into the future, the more you are losing—at an accelerating pace. Invading your capital deprives you of the vast power of having your dollars work for you, silently but relentlessly, through compound-ing. Making such an imprudent error is no less than forfeiture of the opportunity to have the "most powerful force on earth" in your corner, helping you make money effortlessly.

Moreover, since all the dollars that come into your possession are *potential* investment dollars, you must keep their outflow to a mini-mum by preciously saving them in all ways possible. Not to do so is financial suicide. Do you still feel so indifferent about the money you just spent?

(2) Likewise, for the same reason, *avoid debt* if at all possible be-cause with debt comes interest *payment*. Don't ever fail to pay your credit card balance in full within the grace period to avoid those near-usurious interest charges. You may responsibly wish to get a mortgage, for the very real personal benefits of home ownership, but by all means *put as much money down* as you can afford in order to minimize the total debt owed and the mortgage interest payments. Each dollar of inter-est paid takes away a dollar that could have been earning compound interest *for* you. *Paying* interest perverts and transmogrifies (sorry, that

means twists into something grotesque) the benefits of compound interest into a corresponding mirror-image detriment that hits you right away, as well as on into the future, with accelerating impact.

The only way you would want to incur debt from a *financial gain* perspective—a home mortgage is really *consumption* more than investment—is if you could be assured that the return you earn on borrowed dollars will be greater than the interest rate paid for the loan. (Buying on *margin* is the correct term for this. Perhaps you have heard that such a strategy is dangerous.) In other words, borrow at a low rate and reinvest the proceeds at a higher rate. Unfortunately, such sure-fire opportunities are very rare for the individual (as opposed to large financial institutions). To the contrary, this pursuit is very risky. Don't try it. A very prudent general rule to abide by is: avoid debt. If you can't afford something without borrowing, don't buy it. Again, a worthwhile exception may be the home mortgage, depending on your needs. But even with that kind of debt, be aware of, and compute, the total cost over time including interest payments, to see how the true cost dwarfs the stated purchase price and to see what you are really getting yourself into. (We will have more on the practical economics of home ownership and mortgages in Chapter 8.) Frankly, adhere to the principles I am giving you and you may not even need a mortgage. You'll be able to pay cash for a home, as I did, without even wincing.

Manna, or Moolah, from Heaven

How would you like to have $45,000 drop right out of the sky and into your lap? That happened to me, more or less, because I arranged for it to happen. No, not another free car—I got that money by saving and using coupons. Really.

Take a look at Table 5-2(a) which reports my monthly and yearly coupon savings over a fairly recent (by my standards) four-year period. Manufacturer coupons include the kind you clip from the Sunday newspaper insert and redeem at supermarkets and drugstores for the purchase of household goods. As shown in the table, I recorded my total savings

TABLE 5-2(a)

COUPON SAVINGS, 1992-95

	Retail Service	Manufacturer		Retail Service	Manufacturer
01/92	$33.06		01/93	$96.43	
02/92	25.05	$20.69	02/93	32.51	$39.24
03/92	41.32		03/93	29.61	
04/92	85.98	21.01	04/93	30.90	45.36
05/92	31.87		05/93	28.91	
06/92	29.73	21.26	06/93	63.53	40.00
07/92	22.99		07/93	56.34	
08/92	24.62	21.80	08/93	21.81	52.45
09/92	51.78		09/93	12.46	
10/92	66.35	32.51	10/93	17.63	50.13
11/92	40.65		11/93	44.57	
12/92	33.58	56.42	12/93	49.14	54.90
Total	**$486.98**	**$173.69**	**Total**	**$483.84**	**$282.08**

	Retail Service	Manufacturer		Retail Service	Manufacturer
01/94	$25.72		01/95	$78.90	
02/94	26.98	$23.84	02/95	40.13	$28.67
03/94	10.10		03/95	24.76	
04/94	23.33	56.43	04/95	23.70	53.91
05/94	30.19		05/95	28.99	
06/94	57.25	28.00	06/95	63.03	52.03
07/94	20.00		07/95	18.42	
08/94	112.89	52.72	08/95	69.37	41.48
09/94	30.11		09/95	45.66	
10/94	26.54	34.06	10/95	30.45	46.02
11/94	56.29		11/95	44.57	
12/94	25.38	34.89	12/95	49.44	62.10
Total	**$444.78**	**$229.94**	**Total**	**$517.42**	**$284.21**

from these handy and underappreciated little instruments bi-monthly. "Retail *service*" coupons include, primarily, the kind distributed by local service businesses, e.g., restaurants, auto repair and service shops, etc. These savings are totaled per month in 5-2(a) and as you can see in Table 5-2(b), my usage of service coupons is heavily skewed toward fast-food joints. (If that junk food weren't adequately nutritious, the government wouldn't allow it to be sold, would it? It doesn't seem to have stunted my growth or harmed me. I'm about 6'5", 220 lbs. and, not only do I choose to wear the same clothes I wore in college well over a quarter century ago, I *am able* to.) The main reason I present Table 5-2(b), reproducing a sample of my own rough work sheets, is to prove to you that I really did keep track of this apparent minutiae. (Now I'm going to stop doing it, forever. Stop me, please, before I do it again.) The main reason I kept such a record in the first place was sheer curiosity to learn just how much I was saving from coupons. I had no idea it was so much.

Table 5-2(c) contains the 1992-95 annual totals and also reports estimated coupon savings for previous years back to 1976, about the time I would have begun the practice. (I apologize for not recording the value of every store coupon I ever used over the entire 20-year period. For most of that time, I didn't realize I'd be writing this book.) The basis for the estimates is simply this: Take the average yearly total over 1992-95 ($725.74) and *backcast* by adjusting that number for inflation. Using the most common inflation measure, the Cost of Living Index,[8] we adjust downward year by year from the '92-'95 starting point. For example, to get from 1992 to 1985 apply the ratio of the 1985/92 indices (107.8/140.3, from the cited reference book) to the '92 averaged *estimate* ($725.74), yielding $557.60. (We do not bother separating out retail/manufacturer categories in the backcasted estimates.) In other words, all the numbers in the estimated "Total" column are equivalent in real dollars, differing only by the inflation adjustment. From the table, we see that the total estimated plus actual coupon savings in raw, nominal dollars is $11,021.18. Then, we must

TABLE 5-2(b)

COUPON SAVINGS WORKSHEET

Sept. '95	
Hardee's	1.15
Outback Steak	25.—
Steak'n'Shake	.84
Little Caesars	.32
Steak'n'Shake	.80
Bill Knapp's	3.65
Taco Bell	.65
Steak'n'Shake	1.05
Noble Roman's	1.31
Steak'n'Shake	.63
Red Lobster	2.10
Steak'n'Shake	.80
" "	1.12
car wash	1,—
Oyster Bar	1.75
" "	.90
Steak'n'Shake	.84
Little Caesar's	.83
Steak'n'Shake	.92
	45.66

Oct. '95	
Bill Knapp's	1.05
Arby's	1.66
Bill Knapp's	.21
Arby's	1.70
Papa John's pizza	2.20
Arby's	.74
Dairy Queen	1.25
free Egg McMuffin	1.48
free Daily Double burger	1.67
oil change	5.25
Noble Roman's	1.31
free Big Mac	1.88
Noble Roman's	1.31
free Filet o' Fish	1.64
Perkins breakfast	1.59
Oyster Bar	1.00
free 1/4 Pounder w/cheese	1.88
Ponderosa	.53
Red Lobster	2.10
	30.45

Nov. '95	
free Big Mac	1.88
free Filet-O-Fish	1.64
" Daily Double burger	1.67
" Egg McMuffin	1.48
" Sausage "	1.48
Hans Haus	2.—
U-club	5.06
free Daily Double	1.67
Hardee's Frisco	.32
free Filet-O-Fish	1.64
Long John Silver's	.84
Hardee's Frisco Burger	.52
free Big Mac	1.88
" Egg McMuffin	1.48
free 1/4 lb. w/cheese	1.88
" Big Mac	1.88
" Sausage McMuffin	1.48
" 1/4 lb. w/cheese	1.88
" " " "	1.88
" Big Mac	1.88

free McLean deluxe	1.98
" fries	.72
" Daily Double burger	1.67
" soft drink	.83
" Big Mac	1.88
The Landing, dinner	1.05
Oyster Bar drinks	2.00
	44.57

convert to net present value by applying what those dollars would have earned over the years. This time, I use an ultra-conservative estimated return, 5%, knowing how conservatively I have invested. That net present value computation is found in the final column, revealing a total present couponing worth of $17,761.07 as of when the calculation was done, 1996. Add to this figure $1,657.42 from some larger-value coupons redeemed in more recent years (primarily air travel and hotel) that I tracked separately so as not to bias the estimates, and other sporadically-recorded coupon savings between 1995 year-end and this writing ($5,782.66), convert to *2008 present value @ 5%*, and we get a grand total net present value of $42,956.55—all because I clipped and used common everyday coupons! As there surely have been some occasions when I forgot to record coupon use since I began trying to keep track of it, I feel safe in guessing that the true addition to my net worth is probably about *$45,000* because of this practice. It is literally as if $45,000 just fell into my lap. Wouldn't you like for that to happen to you? If this coupon usage required some effort, it probably wouldn't be worth it, but the effort involved is clearly negligible. The only thing I *don't* recommend is keeping a record of coupon use—unless you're planning to write a book.

Some guys flash a roll of bills; I carry a wad of coupons. And I can't imagine why that has never helped me pick up girls.

Incidentally, you may congratulate me on a major financial deal I concluded recently: I got a regular-sized tube of *Gleem* toothpaste for 75c! How? The product item was on sale at the drugstore for $1.00 and I had a 25c coupon that I know had been in my inventory for at least 25-30 years. (I had been biding my time for just the right tactical opportunity.) You should have seen the look I got from the store clerk as she noted the obviously elderly newsprint coupon, which they don't make like that anymore. I wonder what Procter & Gamble, the manufacturer, thought when the retailer redeemed it. You know those things are coded, so P & G would have been aware of when this one was issued.

TABLE 5-2(c)
1976-95 COUPON SAVINGS

1992-95 Actual				Net Present Value,
Year	Retail Service	Manufacturer	Total	1996, @5%
1995	$517.42	$284.21	$801.63	$841.71
1994	444.78	229.94	674.72	743.88
1993	483.84	282.08	765.92	886.65
1992	486.98	173.69	660.67	803.05
('92-'95 avg.)			($725.74)	
1976-91 Estimated				
1991			$704.98	$899.75
1990			675.53	905.27
1989			641.21	902.25
1988			611.65	903.69
1987			588.01	912.20
1986			566.76	923.19
1985			557.60	953.69
1984			538.45	966.98
1983			515.90	972.81
1982			499.95	989.87
1981			471.27	979.74
1980			425.89	929.66
1979			374.97	859.44
1978			337.76	812.86
1977			313.80	792.95
1976			294.51	781.43
Total			**$11,021.18**	**$17,761.07**

Ironically and coincidentally, as I was manually compiling the tables of numbers you saw in Chapter 2, I noticed my little roll of coupons on the desk next to my work paper. Yes, I did take note of the natural connection between the two. It is largely because of the coupons, more especially my tendency to appreciate them, that I have gained those Chapter 2 wealth amounts.

You probably have not had sufficient appreciation for the lowly store coupon prior to this. You probably haven't appreciated supermarkets enough either. Please allow me one more economic-ideological aside— on the supermarket!

Think of it. The average supermarket contains about 25,000-30,000 different product items, if you count different sizes as different items, as the supermarket industry does (8000-10,000 items if you don't). Do you think it's easy to get 25,000 different products, from thousands of different manufacturers, into your local neighborhood store, and *everybody's* convenient local store? Think of all the tasks that must be performed between manufacture and the retailer to get all those products onto the store shelves, conveniently arrayed for virtually effortless shopping by you. Think of all the transportation, storage, sorting, and assorting, i.e., the primary distribution functions that have to be carried out, as well as support services like billing, payment, collection, financing, risk-taking, and communication that also go on. What our modern distribution system provides is a level of customer convenience literally unimaginable in most parts of the world. Let me tell you a true story about that.

A few years back, when there was still a Soviet Union, one of their MiG fighter pilots flew his jet to Japan and defected to the West, coming to the United States shortly thereafter. An old college buddy of mine (yes, another one), who was employed as an analyst at the Central Intelligence Agency, was part of a task force that was given the assignment of "de-briefing" the young pilot. One of my friend's roles was to help the Soviet airman get acclimated to his new country by taking him around the Washington, DC area and showing him the sights. My friend gave him the full treatment, exposing him to both the exotic and commonplace, but as he later told me, the one that overwhelmed the Russian flier the most was the supermarket. He just couldn't believe there really existed a store with such a grand selection of consumer goods. He was convinced the supermarket was a sham, staged by the CIA to impress foreign visitors. My buddy says they had to visit about four or five stores before his guest could comprehend that there really are such institutions in our country. If you would ever have seen the miserable facsimiles for food stores there were in the old Soviet Union, as I did, you would understand why the average Russian citizen could not fathom the life that American consumers take for granted. Aside from the scarcity or unavailability of many basic products, we could spend the rest of the day on the atrocious product quality all the Eastern Bloc socialist economies were notorious for.

A few years prior to the episode just recounted, the politician Adlai Stevenson, Jr. (the guy who ran against Eisenhower, dated actress Lauren Bacall, and later became U.N. Ambassador) made a remark rather slanderous of his country. He said, "Why should the other peoples of the world want to be like us? What symbols or institutions do we have to hold up to other nations to make them want to emulate us? After all, the supermarket is our temple, the singing commercial our anthem." In response to such defamatory tripe, I will not bother to defend the American TV or radio advertising jingle, though I easily could. (If advertisers knew of a more efficient way of communicating with their customers, to transmit needed information about products, wouldn't they be using it?) The *supermarket*, however, is a highly appropriate symbol of our wondrous economic system, symbolizing and contributing to a level of consumer affluence, convenience, and abundance that most consumers on the planet can only dream of. As I tell my marketing students, every time you enter a supermarket you should *genuflect*, out of reverence for the miracle of distribution, and economic blessing, those "temples of capitalism" represent. You too, Adlai.

While we are on the subject of the majesty of our economic system, did you know that the average income (and living standard) of Americans living *below the official poverty level* is higher than that of (a) the average *person* in the remaining socialist countries, (b) the average person in a *majority* of the world's countries, and (c) the average of all people world-wide? That is true. In other words, what we consider poverty in the United States would be known as affluence and luxury in most parts of the world. "Poverty" exists in the United States primarily because we *define it* as being present. By absolute standards, by global standards, and based on the above evidence, there is *almost no* genuine poverty in the U.S. (Our official poverty rate of 10-12% does not take into account some government transfer payments, "underground" un-reported income, or low-*income* retirees who have substantial *wealth*. If it did, the rate would be about 3%.) Perhaps this reality is related in some way to the fact that you can actually get rich in this country with-out even having to make very much money! It definitely is attributable to the huge amount of wealth our economy generates in the aggregate. Is this a great country or what? And all these wonders are accomplished despite the low national savings rate, as elaborated earlier. Just think how great things will be if we can boost that rate a little through our saving efforts.

Chapter 6

Back to Basics: A Compendium of Money-Saving Tips
(If You're Ready for This)

We've all known people who would boast about how *much* they paid for conspicuous consumption items. In recent years, by contrast, a cottage industry of what might be called "frugality self-help publications" has emerged as a counterforce to that mentality. This wise vanguard of the "frugal chic" movement advances the idea that the opposite orientation, a *sensible* spending approach, is more, well, sensible—and cool! In Chapter 4 I referenced the book by Robin and Dominguez. There also are some periodicals and blogs that regularly transmit tips on how to save money. Here, for your potential enlightenment and consideration, is a list[1] of some of the more prominent entries of this genre:

THE TIGHTWAD GAZETTE
(*Promoting Thrift as a Viable Alternative Lifestyle*)
RR1, Box 3570
Leeds, ME 04263
One year/12 issues: $12
(www.fiassociates.org/resource)

CHEAPSKATE MONTHLY
(*Bringing Dignity to the Art of Living Within One's Means*)
P.O. Box 2135
Paramount, CA 90723
One year/12 issues: $15.95
(www.debtproofliving.com)

SKINFLINT NEWS
P.O. Box 818
Palm Harbor, FL 34682
One year/12 issues: $9.95

THE PENNY PINCHER
(*Save Smart, Live Better*)
P.O. Box 809
Kings Park, NY 11754
One year/12 issues: $15
(www.geocities.com/RodeoDrive/4015)

LIVING CHEAP NEWS
(*Promoting Practical Parsimony*)
7232 Belleview
Kansas City, MO 64114
One year/10 issues: $12
(www.livingcheap.com)

THE CHEAPSKATE REPORT
(*The Guide to Frugal Living*)
P.O. Box 394
Antioch, CA 94509
One year/10 issues: $9.95

Though I have seldom actually seen any of these publications—I don't exactly need any help to be able to save money—based upon what I have learned from news accounts, I can give you the flavor of their reputed content. In fairness, we should approach these sources as frugality brainstorming sessions. Not all the ideas they "run up the flagpole" will be appealing, but these newsletters and websites do constitute a repository of suggestions from which to choose. Common fare seems to be standard advice like buy used instead of new, buy in bulk, shop yard sales, do comparison shopping in general, grow a vegetable garden, car pool, and reuse and wear out the products you do own, e.g., keep your car a year longer. Some of the more drastic pointers I've seen include: bake your own bread, form baby-sitting cooperatives with friends and relatives, wrap Christmas presents in leftover wallpaper, and convert clothes-dryer lint to fire starter.[2] Before anyone begins to think I am like the film critic who relies on second-hand testimony about movies, let us clarify that the purpose of this review is only to allow you to decide if you wish to explore these sources further.

From time to time, money-saving advice for consumer households is carried in major outlets in the general media. The sampling of such material I have collected for this report, as follows, may fairly represent the main body of knowledge on the subject. First, from the esteemed *Chicago Tribune*'s financial section:[3]

• Ever notice how quickly shirt collars wear out? Instead of throwing away a shirt that is otherwise good, take it to a dry cleaner and have the collar turned. A tailor can do the job for less than $5.

• When you buy fruit or vegetables that are pre-bagged, they usually are sold by weight. A 5-pound bag, for example, means the bag contains "at least" 5 pounds. Some bags may weigh slightly more. By weighing a few bags, it may be possible to get an extra pound—a 20 percent bonus—for the same price.

• The next time you go out to dinner, skip dessert.

• When traveling on vacation, you can save on hotel costs by staying with friends or relatives.

• To slash your long-distance phone bills, make an outline of all the things you want to discuss before you make a call—then stick to it.

• Fruit juice may cost several dollars a bottle, and some children can run through an entire bottle in a single day. When you buy juice, pour it into a large container and mix it with a good portion of water. Most children would never notice.

• Bring your lunch to work.

• Reduce insurance premiums by taking larger deductibles.

• Buy energy-efficient appliances that not only are cheaper in the long-run but also help conserve energy.

• Drop expensive "add-on" services you can easily do without, such as extra features on your telephone.

• Take full advantage of coupon and refund offers, but do not buy anything you do not need.

• Shop the grocery stores and wholesale clubs that save you the best combination of money and time.

• Look at your car only as a contraption to take you from Point A to Point B, not as a status symbol.

• Drive smartly and defensively, keeping to the speed limit, and avoid jack-rabbit starts and sudden stops.

• Color-coordinate your wardrobe to save on shoes and other accessories.

• Do not shop on impulse, or because you are bored, but make a list of the things you need, and stick to it.

• Quit smoking if you smoke, and do not start if you do not smoke.

• Every now and then, try a vacation at home.

• Shop around for the best deal among banks and savings and loans, and don't keep your money in low-interest, high-fee checking accounts.

• Take care of yourself. Keep in good health—to save on medical bills.

• Don't pay credit card annual fees, unless the card offers rebates that offset the cost. If your card issuer won't waive the fee, find another company.

• Don't renew your auto insurance without shopping around to see if you can get a better deal.

• Do protest your property tax assessment. Your house may be worth less than it was four or five years ago. If your tax assessment hasn't been adjusted, you may be paying too much.

Perhaps the most legendary of all personal finance columnists, Jane Bryant Quinn, offers you these ideas:[4]

• Lie to yourself. Hide money in places you're not likely to plunder, such as a distant bank by mail.

• Lie to your significant other. Let your check register show $300 less than is really in your account so your spouse won't wring the balance dry.

• Don't spend small checks. Put every check for birthday gifts, stock dividends and minor health-insurance reimbursements into savings.

• Save each day's change.

• Save small cash payments, such as the $10 a friend borrowed last week. You've gotten along without it so far, so it could easily be saved.

• Start a "No" account. If you try on a sweater, then decide not to buy it, write a check for the cost and put it into savings.

• Hold a tag sale. You won't believe what some people will pay good money for.

• Save bonuses and raises. If you got by on $30,000 last year, you can do the same this year—and bank your 3.5 percent ($1,050) raise. You can increase your payroll deduction by an amount equal to the raise.

Over the years, *Woman's Day* magazine has carried at least 292 money-saving suggestions, including those from J. B. Quinn, above. (No, I don't read that magazine. Mom passes this material along to you through her son, who doesn't even take *Sports Illustrated*, *Business Week*, or *Golf Digest*—not willing to pay the subscription price. I do have a complimentary subscription to *The Wall Street Journal*.) I will not reprint all 292, but here are some highlights.[5]

• Buy products that come with good warranties from retailers who stand behind what they sell.

• Now that movies hit the shelves in video-rental stores and libraries so quickly, it hardly pays to add $10 or more to your monthly cable bill for special movie channels.

• Buy generic or store brands

• Take along a calculator when you shop and check unit prices to make sure you're getting the most for your money.

• Check the top and bottom shelves at grocery stores for less-expensive brands.

• The large economy-size isn't necessarily the best value if perishables will spoil before you use them up.

• Save your receipts and return any unsatisfactory purchases.

• Buy at the beginning or end of the season for the greatest discounts.

• Arrange for regular bills to be paid automatically by your bank. It saves the cost of envelopes, stamps, and checks.

• Check all bills for overcharges, duplications and other mistakes.

• Don't give the Internal Revenue Service a free loan. If you receive a large refund each year, you're losing interest on the money. It pays to lower your withholding and bank the difference.

• Buy personal checks from a discount service instead of your bank. They are advertised in the Sunday newspaper inserts.

• Do your own income tax returns. It's not that hard.

• Check out the public clinics in your area. You may qualify for some free or low-cost medical services.

• Add a few ounces of hot water to almost-finished shampoo and detergent bottles to make them last longer.

• Save cardboard boxes and plastic filler for future mailings of your own.

• Use prestamped postcards, instead of letters, for short messages.

• Barter your services for others you need.

• If everyone sold the exercise equipment that is gathering dust in basements, we could probably pay off the national debt. Buy used equipment, or rent before you buy, to be sure you'll stick with the program.

• Everything goes on sale eventually. Either wait for the sale, negotiate a lower price, buy directly from the manufacturer or shop at discount stores.

Now, some of the *Woman's Day* tips arranged by category:

ENTERTAINING

• Have drinks and cocktails at home before eating out, or come back home for dessert and coffee.

• When you're eating out, order an appetizer, or soup and salad, instead of an entree.

• Meet a friend for a brisk walk instead of going to a restaurant during your lunch hour.

• Go to matinees instead of evening movies. They're often discounted.

• Many restaurants allow adults to order from the lower-priced kids' menu. If you lack the appetite or budget, give it a try.

• Patronize restaurants that offer "kids eat free" nights.

• Order ice water with a slice of lemon instead of soda or other restaurant beverages.

• Share one large entree with your dinner date and order an extra salad to fill out the meal.

• Take advantage of slack-period discounts at restaurants. The meal that costs $20 at 7 P.M. may be only $10 at noon or at 5 P.M.

• Take your own candy or popcorn when you go to the movies.

• Share video rentals with neighbors.

• If you're served more food in a restaurant than you can eat, don't waste it; ask to have the left-overs wrapped to be taken home.

• Pass up vending machines, coffee carts and snack bars when you take a break at work. Bring snacks from home and, if possible, make your own coffee.

• Share brown-bag lunches with a co-worker. If you each make two lunches every other day (or week), it's easier.

• Ask local colleges, community centers, churches, museums and parks departments to send you notices of free or low-cost events.

• Visit your public library for more than just books. Some branches loan audio and video and even works of art.

ENERGY AND ELECTRICITY

• Reduce your water-heater temperature from 145° to 120° and you'll reduce water-heating costs by 10 to 15 percent.

• During winter months, open drapes during the day to take advantage of solar energy, then close them at night to help retain the heat.

• Stop leaks by weather-stripping, caulking and insulating. Replacing storm windows or covering windows with plastic film can save 2 to 7 percent on heating costs.

• Never leave the water running while brushing teeth, washing hair or doing the dishes.

• Fix leaky faucets in the kitchen and bathroom. One drop per second can waste eight gallons of water a week.

• Save 10 cents to 20 cents per wash by using the air-dry or energy-saver cycle on your dishwasher.

• Take advantage of off-peak electric rates.

• Install fluorescent bulbs in fixtures that stay on for long periods; they produce four times as much light per watt as incandescent bulbs and last 10 times as long.

• Put low-watt bulbs in lamps not used for reading.

• Unplug instant-on, remote-control television sets when you go away. These models continue to draw electricity even when turned off.

• Avoid heating an iron to press one garment. You'll save electricity if you iron a pile of clothes at once—and turn off the iron before you're actually finished.

• Prepare as many meals as possible with energy-saving appliances, such as a microwave oven, a pressure cooker or a Crock-Pot.

• Cook several dishes together in your oven; an extra roast or casserole can be frozen and reheated later.

• Turn off the water heater when your house is empty—whether for a weekend or a week's vacation.

• Limit your use of exhaust fans. They suck out cool air in summer and heat in winter.

• Wash all but the most soiled clothes in warm or even cold water. This saves the average family $50 a year.

• Run your dishwasher only when full, likewise with your washer and dryer.

• Turn your refrigerator to a warmer setting when you go away.

• Use warm nightclothes and bedcovers so you can turn the heat down low on cold winter nights.

• Set thermostats at 68º or less in winter, 78º or more in summer.

• Close off unused rooms in winter.

• Train your family to conserve water by taking short showers instead of baths.

• Avoid watering your lawn or garden at midday when the sun causes water to evaporate.

CLOTHING

• Change your clothes as soon as you get home from work or social events to minimize the chance of stains and snags.

• Ask your favorite factory outlets and discount stores to put you on their mailing lists.

• Search thrift shops, resale stores, and other secondhand outlets.

• Arrange a clothing swap with friends. [Some of these suggestions are obviously directed more at women than men.]

• Ask store managers for discounts on soiled or flawed merchandise.

• Save up to 55 percent on name-brand pantyhose and lingerie by ordering imperfects or seconds from the factory. [Some of these suggestions are *really* obviously directed more at women than men.]

- Add metal tips to heels of shoes to minimize wear.
- Study care labels before you buy, primarily to avoid the high cost of dry cleaning.
- Spray clothes that are easily stained with fabric protector.

AUTOMOBILE AND TRAVEL-RELATED

- Drive a new car off the lot and it loses a certain percent of its value. Do your homework and you can buy a car that's next to new for a fraction of the original sticker price.
- Change your own oil every 3000 miles, and take the used oil to a quick-lube facility for recycling.
- Maintain proper tire pressure.
- Wash your car often, especially in winter, to avoid rust and expensive paint jobs.
- Buy parts through auto-recycling or auto-salvage yards, usually at a price reduction of 50 percent or more.
- Use public transportation.
- Find a mechanic you can trust for car maintenance and repairs.
- Drop expensive collision insurance on older cars.
- Don't discuss the trade-in value of your old car until you've agreed on the price for the new one.
- When traveling during the summer or holidays, check with colleges to see if they rent out dorm rooms.
- Buy regular gas, and pump your own. Few cars need premium today.
- Buy oil and wiper-fluid in auto or discount stores and replace it yourself.
- To save fuel, do not let the car idle or drive at speeds above 55 mph. Maintain steady speeds.
- Study a map to see if you can avoid toll roads without increasing driving time.
- Keep a set of jumper cables in your trunk.
- Ask about using reconditioned or secondhand parts for repairs.

• Consider buying retreads or blemished tires, especially for an older car. You can save up to 50 percent.

• Combine errands and exercise, i.e., a walk, and skip driving entirely.

• Get your air filter cleaned and have the wheel alignment checked regularly, for better mileage.

THE HOME

• Reupholster or slipcover furniture instead of replacing it.

• Use old rags and socks for cleaning instead of paper towels.

• Spray fabric protector on new furniture, car upholstery and carpets.

• Try using half the usual amount of detergent in the dishwasher.

• Recycle damaged goods. A blanket can be sewn into pillow covers, for example.

• Arrange joint purchases of garden tools and household equipment—such as lawn mowers and floor polishers—with friends and neighbors.

• Learn to make minor repairs. "How To" books are in the public library.

• Look for seconds, imperfects, and discontinued styles in sheets, towels, glassware, and other household supplies.

• Shop at thrift shops, garage sales and secondhand stores for good buys on basic tools and accessories—such as rakes, lamps, bookcases, desks.

It may have seemed like 292, but it was only 104! As one of the compilers of this listing, R. E. Greer, expresses it,

Some of the methods . . . are too time consuming—or downright embarrassing—even for me, but that's O.K. The key to successful penny pinching is to make it as painless as possible. . . . This collection of money-savers is designed to give you a choice. I don't use them all, and neither should you. Just pick your favorites—and have fun with the money you save.[6]

I recall a feature I saw in *Mad Magazine* only about forty-five years ago. (That was the last magazine I read regularly, I believe, and we sure have cited a variety of sources here, haven't we?) The feature presented, in cartoon form, the distinction between *normal* nonconformists (called "beatniks" at the time, remember?) and *Mad* nonconformists. Analogously, if the frugality advice just listed represents the normal, mainstream thinking on the subject, what follows may be considered the extreme, lunatic-fringe, *Mad* counterculture wing of the penny-pincher world. First, some reader suggestions solicited and reported by a *Chicago Tribune* financial columnist:[7]

• Looking to save money on paper towels and toilet tissue? Buy the two-ply brands, and separate the layers as you go. A single roll will last longer.

• Women: Are you tired of throwing out pantyhose with a run in one leg? Buy more than one pair in the same style and color. When one leg gets a run, cut it off. Do the same when a second pair of hose is damaged. Then, when you have two pairs of one-legged pantyhose, slip them on together.

• To re-use a vacuum cleaner bag, unroll the glued bottom to open and shake out the dirt. The end is rolled again and stapled. Make sure you use enough staples.

• What can you do with all those tiny soap chips that accumulate in the shower? Collect them in a non-stick container and melt them in a microwave. The liquid can then be poured into a mold to make a new bar.

• Next time you finish a loaf of bread, save the plastic bag. Chop off the top part and use the bottom as a sandwich bag. You can even use the wire twist to keep your sandwich fresh.

• Greeting cards can be expensive. Therefore, agree with friends and relatives not to sign the cards you exchange. That way, they can be reused—provided you don't send a card back to the original sender.

• Or, if a greeting card has been signed on one side, chop off that part and use the other half as a postcard. Leave room for the stamp.

• Look for treasure in another man's trash. Watch your neighbors' curbs to see what they throw out.

• Instead of throwing away used paper plates, use them as dishes for your pets.

I probably shouldn't do this in public, but I think I can top some of those.

• As I write this, I look around my home and realize that almost everything I own I did not pay for! Not only the clothes (over 150 shirts, not including tee-shirts, and 100 pair of pants in total, mostly ripened college wardrobe, more recent gifts, or won in golf outings, none of which I purchased) and the '97 car in the garage, but almost all the furniture is hand-me-downs from my folks that Goodwill probably would not accept. ("I'll put my money in the bank, not on the floor.") The tee-shirt I am wearing is the one issued to me in freshman phys ed class, during my freshman year of *high school* in 1963! That thing is indestructible. They don't make them like that any more.

Oh, let's go into the kitchen. . . . Utensils, pots, pans, china—all ancient surplus donated by my parents. (As I've acknowledged, their saving record is, in reality, more impressive than it appears on paper, mine slightly less.) Almost everything else is some kind of commercial premium or freebie. Corporate logos or trademarks decorating cups and glasses in the kitchen cupboard include McDonald's, Folger's, Hiram Walker, Heineken, Chicago Cubs, Chicago Bears, Notre Dame, Churchill Downs, South Bend Country Club, Needham's Business Machines, WSBT Radio, NASA, the Shi-Kay Lounge, Pat's Colonial Pub, Andrean High School, and Gurley-Leep Buick—a perfectly matching set, as far as I am concerned. If anybody doesn't like it, that's their problem. I did purchase all the (minimal) food, but that leads us in another direction.

• Aside from a heavy proportion of ultra-low cost fast food in the diet, I do take advantage of every free meal opportunity that comes along. Official business dinners that most people try to duck, and I'm there. I've become renowned for it. Why not?—I'm a bachelor. The price is right. Call me "America's guest." I've even learned to appreciate airline food! Here's how: Just make sure you are always *very hungry* when you get on a plane, and then you can hardly wait for that cart to come around. In fact, your mission of getting rich without making very much money seems pretty easy compared to organizing airline meal service, doesn't it?

• As I look in my desk drawer, I know that the next letters I write will be on stationery from the Holiday Inn—Kennedy Space Center (which I visited in 1996), the San Francisco Hilton (which has to be from 1988), or the Hotel Pribaltiyskaya (in the city known as Leningrad when I was there in 1982). Very recently, I finally used up my supply from the Twelve Caesars hotel in Miami Beach, where I stayed one weekend in 1973! (No, I don't have any hotel towels, although I was falsely accused of lifting one at the Hotel Cosmos in Moscow—just a way the old Soviets had of shaking down tourists for hard currency. And you wouldn't believe how little that eight-day trip to Russia in 1982 cost me: about $1000.) I have yet to use up the extra mustard and sugar packets I picked up on the 1996 Florida trip. Maybe I'll throw something away for once, probably the mustard.

Do I spend a lot on travel? No, almost all of it is professional business travel to present papers at academic conferences, paid for by my employer. I used to average about four or five trips a year, invariably down South during the winter. I have specialized in business travel to pleasant, resort locales. Most academics do the same, to a large extent, though probably wouldn't admit it.

I glance at the used envelope on my desk, hand-labeled "2007 tax receipts," and notice its postmark is from 1981. The lesson: Don't ever throw anything away if you might be able to use it some day.

• Of course I steam unused stamps off envelopes when I have the chance. The irony of the most recent such occasion struck me.

It was a stamped reply envelope for a university function. Since I could drop it in on-campus, versus U.S., mail, the stamp was not necessary. Free first class stamp for me, therefore.

The university occasion in question was a recognition dinner for all major donors of endowed scholarships. Many years ago I arranged for the testamentary estates of my parents and me to be donated to my school, after we pass on, to establish a scholarship fund for needy and deserving students, and that is why we qualified for the invitation. (That is also how I got a *free* plat in the Notre Dame cemetery, which happens to be adjacent to the campus golf course. As I tell my friends, I insisted on good visibility, right next to the drive landing area for the 16th hole. I want my epitaph, preferably in neon lights, to read: "I hit my tee shot in here so many times, I decided I might as well stay permanently," or "I'm here looking for my lost ball," or "I told them I was sick." [After this writing, author's epitaph, but not the author himself, was finalized: "Ironically, I rest where my drive on old #16 often did: out of bounds."] Since you've got me on this morbid topic, I can't resist one more. On the back of my driver's license, in the space provided for specifying any organs you wish to donate, it reads, "Anything you want, as long as you're sure I'm dead.")

Oh yes, steaming stamps off envelopes. I'm standing over the stove doing just that and I realize we are paying about $2 million for that invitation, essentially (the current value, as of then, of our future donation), and here I am trying to save a lousy 40 cents. But there is a lesson embedded in that juxtaposition, too:

One day I was on the phone with one of the investment companies I deal with, trying to beat them out of a few dollars or a few cents. Basically I was trying to either renew an investment note or redeem it for cash, I forget which, in a way that didn't cause me to lose even a day's worth of interest. The customer service rep told me, politely, "If I had $10,000 [the principal amount of the investment], I wouldn't be worrying about a few days' worth of interest." My equally polite response to her was, "It is precisely *because* I am concerned about small amounts of money that I have large amounts of money."

That is the relevant principle. Never overlook or fail to appreciate the small amounts because, over time and through compounding, they *become* large amounts. Take good care of the small amounts and they will take care of you by becoming large amounts.

A few years ago I was sitting in our favorite bar with my girlfriend at the time (yes, another one), as it was becoming obvious that the honeymoon was over and I was really starting to get on her nerves. After buying a round, I was meticulously putting my folding money back into my wallet, making sure all those ex-presidents were perfectly straightened and facing the same way, so they would be comfortable and happy. Observing this excessive ritual, my friend snapped at me, "Who gives a _ _ _ _?" My response to her was, "If you're nice to them, and treat them with respect, they'll be nice to you." I can't imagine why we broke up soon after that.

- "He never buys anything." Not quite true; of course I have to buy some things. I just buy fewer things than almost anyone else because I don't give a damn about most of the things people buy, and I also endeavor to spend less on the things I do have to buy. For example, concerning the custom of tipping, where did this idea of a standard 15% service charge come from, let alone 20%? Those people already are receiving wages. If it's a quality restaurant with adequate service, fine. For the lower-quality dives, I mean diners, like most of us have occasionally patronized in the interest of economy, the upper end of the scale should be proportionally lower, say 10%. Then, if *anything* goes wrong, if there is any deficiency in food or service, the gratuity should be reduced. If a major lapse occurs, and it is the server's responsibility, tip is forfeited. This game's easy.

If restaurant customers weren't so tolerant, and enforced more of a merit- and quality-based system, service would improve immeasurably. Wait-personnel in public establishments have become complacent, generally, because of the weakening of the direct connection between their performance and their reward. This needs to be rectified. I'm doing my part. As you would expect, I am well-known and not appreciated by some restaurant personnel in my home town. They confuse cause and effect. They started it; I didn't. Don't do anything wrong and you get

10-15% with no argument from me. Don't get me started. (See, I don't believe everything about this country is perfect.)

Of course, I never order a beverage other than water with a restaurant meal. I can have a much lower-cost cup of coffee when I get home or a free one at the faculty lounge. Oh sure, I may have a few beers later on.

That's the idea, you see. Prioritize. Your priorities will likely be very different from mine, but you must set them. Minimize expenditure on those things that are not important to you, and you will have plenty of money available for the things that are.

Eccentric? Who, me? It paid off, didn't it? Instead of eccentricity, think of these measures as proper antagonism toward waste of precious resources. You got a problem with that? If so, I think *you're* strange. And you haven't seen anything yet.

• I didn't visit a barber for 14 years, which saved me a few dollars. In the spring of 1969, before returning home following my sophomore year in college, I got a haircut because my father had informed me that he wouldn't allow me in the house if I didn't. Never a "hippie," but I looked that way to him. My next paid haircut was in 1983, after I had already been a university professor for a few years.

What did I do in the meantime? I cut my own hair. Not very well, but the price was right. How hard can it be? Pull it back wet, chop it off. Pull it down on the sides, chop it off again. Same in front—you're done. It didn't look very good, I am sure, but I'm not running for office. Finally, though, I did tire of my amateur hair and that was when I resumed interaction with commercial hair-cutters.

By that time, 1983, they were already known as "hair stylists" instead of barbers, so I knew I was in for a new experience. After we had completed the neo-virginal act, my first good haircut in 14 years, I asked the hair service provider "How much?" When she said "seven," I honestly didn't know if that meant seven dollars or seven hundred, so out of touch with that industry was I. If the price had turned out to be the latter (in fact, it was the former), I would have written a check and not given it a thought. I just would never have gotten another haircut.

Now I'm getting hair transplants—for free, from a golf buddy who is a dermatologist. I'm volunteering to be his demonstration and practice case.

Incidentally, the estimated net present value to me, right now, of not having gone to a barber for 14 years in the long ago is approximately $1,996.73, by my rough calculations.

• I used toilet paper instead of Kleenex (but never the converse) until I had over a quarter million dollars. Didn't think I could afford the better stuff. (I'm assuming toilet paper is less expensive per use than tissue paper. Gee, I hope I didn't make a mistake.)

• I play a lot of golf, but I never buy golf balls. I haven't bought a golf ball in longer than I can remember—it must be at least 40 years—because I don't need to. I have a lifetime supply primarily as a result of my father's wisdom.

One of the better investments Dad ever made was his purchase of a golf ball retriever, the kind that allows you to fish balls out of water hazards. (Or did he get that thing for free?) He has snagged so many near-mint condition balls over the decades, just during rounds of golf as he continues to do, that he has provided us with an endless supply. Really, along with other sources such as boxes of balls received as favors at golf outings and five dozen a good friend gave me as a Ph.D.-graduation gift, I've got a closet full, probably more than I'll ever be able to use—but I'll try. By the way, those old golf balls don't go stale, do they?

Yet I still use my golf equipment as judiciously as possible. Our pro at South Bend Country Club is amazed at how old my clubs are (1974 Ping irons, a gift from my parents) and the fact that I never need to buy anything from the pro shop. When I happened to win the A-Flight of the city golf tournament in 1995, the most newsworthy aspect reported in the *South Bend Tribune* the next day was the odd fact that I had used the same ball for *both* of the final two rounds. The *Trib* reporter thought that was unheard of; most players will change balls every six holes in tournament competition. (Apparently it didn't harm my performance. I shot 73 in the fourth and final round, after a 76 in the third. And I'd rather not reveal most of my more recent scores.)

Aren't you getting sick and tired of hearing how good I have it, how blessed and lucky I've been? Free cars, clothes, home furnishings, meals, travel, even orthodontia, medical services, a cemetery plat, and now golf balls—one could just gag! It should be obvious, though, that it hasn't all been luck. You have to be alert to opportunities. I really believe my life-long dedication to freebies has produced at least $200,000 in present net worth for me, probably a quarter million. Now do you understand?

I do not disclose all this personal information gratuitously or ca-priciously, however. There is a reason for it. I am hoping some reader will be inspired by those numbers I report (the ones with the dollar signs), to achieve the same success. Those numbers could be yours. I'm only hoping that some of the mentality and attitude that have produced wealth far in excess of what I have earned will rub off, beneficially, on some readers. The only people I'm trying to impress are those who have nothing, didn't think they ever *could* have anything, and are beginning to realize that they *can* achieve something—without even making very much money.

• Beyond securing a limitless supply of free golf balls, my father's (and mother's) contributions to the theory and practice of frugality would fill another book, so I'll just give you some of the exclamation points that would punctuate that volume.

When my father was in the hospital recently for major surgery, his paramount concern, at least overtly, was getting his medicine at the lowest possible price—even though insurance paid for most of it. His first words upon returning home: "Did any checks come in the mail?"

I still visit my parents about once a month, and while having dinner at their home on one recent occasion, I noticed my father, after having finished his salad, pouring the watery remains of his French dressing back into the bottle for future reuse. Admirable spirit which I can cer-tainly endorse but, since then, my mother and I have made sure that he has his own *personal* bottle of French salad dressing.

It did not surprise me to learn that my parents produce their own home-made pancake syrup, reusing and reusing an old Mrs. Butterworth's bottle that has been around for many years.

Just a few years ago, as my father was removing a shirt from the commercial laundry wrapper, he remarked, "Cery Cleaners?! I haven't been there since I lived at 4th & Washington (in Gary) before we were married. That was *1942*." Yes, his shirt had been sitting at the bottom of a drawer, or various drawers, folded and wrapped, for over half a century—literally, almost 60 years! It was well-creased, but clean, when he then wore it.

• Throughout most of my college years I would dye my moustache green on St. Patrick's Day, using food coloring. Another conversation-piece stunt. What some guys won't do.

This past Easter I noticed that my 90-year-old mother is still using that same bottle of green food coloring to decorate her Easter eggs—40 years after my purchase and first use of it. Why not? Why discard value? That stuff doesn't spoil. Have that attitude and grow rich!

Again, emphatically, to avoid leaving the wrong impression, my parents' penny-pinching proclivities were, and are, anything but mercenary and coarse. Their thrifty qualities are charming, endearing, uplifting, maybe quaint, and decidedly perspicacious and effective (see Tables 2-2 and 2-3). My father came up the hard way in the Gary, Indiana steel mill and never had a pot to spit in, so to speak, so he's especially entitled. Remember my mother's $2,300 teacher's salary. I guess you would have had to be there in the case of the French dressing, but the acorn doesn't fall too far from the oak tree, does it?

A couple of final illustrations represent more serious information than may first be apparent.

• I opened my first checking account at the age of *ten* (with my parents as co-signatories, legally). The bank president was my father's regular golf partner, so he arranged an exception for us. My parents' motivation was to teach me financial responsibility by giving me some. Mine was the normal one for maintaining "demand deposits": transactional convenience, though I probably couldn't have pronounced it then. What kind of transactions did I write checks for as a ten-year-old?—mail order purchase of comic books, baseball cards, electric train accessories, science fiction books, and a gift for my mother. I believe my parents' purpose was accomplished. I suspect early appreciation and understanding of money had much to do with the fuller, more productive understanding and appreciation (and preoccupation?) that led directly to my eventual success at getting rich without making very much money. Or maybe it all stems from my first savings account, opened for me before I was a year old.

Readers who are parents or prospective parents, if this makes any sense to you I hope you will do something similar for your children. It doesn't have to be a joint checking account at the age of ten, but I hope you can do something to help teach your children the value of a dollar. Maybe an allowance that they have to work for, or a requirement that part of their allowance be saved and later invested, would get the job done. As you have seen, the payoff for them, and the positive impact on their financial lives, can be staggering.

Incidentally, was I the kind of kid who always won at Monopoly? No, I invariably *lost* because I was unwilling to part with my Monopoly money to buy a hotel. I wanted the money more than I wanted the hotel. Haven't changed much? Actually, while in college, I was a spendthrift. So you can change, too. If I can re-train or re-program myself, easily, to do what was not so natural for me, you can too.

• Over three decades ago I was setting into motion the chain of events, the mechanism, that would ensure my eventually getting rich the easiest way most people have available to them. I was also spending a fair amount of time at the Fife & Drum Pub in Lowell, Indiana, drinking beer with friends including an old high school and college classmate who was just starting medical school. Of necessity, since I was just about to start my business doctoral program, we were both motivated to scrimp and conserve. For a time we would sort of compete, to see who could come up with the most extreme examples of penny-pinching behavior, vying for the hypothetical title of "tightest man in America." Sounds like a real barrel of laughs, doesn't it? Talk about *madcap high-jinks* from two *wild and crazy guys*. That's what our drinking buddies thought, too. (Of course, we exempted beer drinking from the frugality contest.) But we knew, if others didn't, that what we were really doing was instilling the right kind of tendencies in ourselves that would ultimately, naturally, and inevitably lead to real wealth. Moreover, I guarantee we both were more financially comfortable during the coming professional studies years than we otherwise would have been.

My friend is now a rich orthopedic surgeon, so he did it primarily the other way, by making money. "Tightest Person in America"? I like to think I won, but I would be glad to surrender the title to you.

Chapter 7

Uncommon Advice on Getting Rich *Fast*

When we offer the prospect of getting rich fast, does this mean "get rich quick" schemes? No, and sort of.

The "get rich quick" approach, as it is commonly understood, would involve *making* a large amount of money and thus would violate our condition of *without* having to make very much money, by definition. (The approach I have outlined delivers *pretty substantial* wealth *fairly* quickly, *reasonably* fast, after *a few* years—e.g., five to eight years at the most, per Tables 2-2, 2-3, 2-7, and 2-9. That's good enough for me and it should be good enough for most people.) If the *relatively* rapid wealth achievement that is possible with our program is not fast enough for you, then let us slightly broaden the interpretation of "without making very much money." We can construe that condition as indicating "without earning a high *wage or salary* income," so getting rich "quick" by other means would still qualify as being faithful to, and within the definitional domain of, the book's title and theme. Let me get away with skating around this technicality that way, please, and we can move on to more interesting matters.

The basic rule to apply when considering any "get rich quick scheme" (hereafter "GRQS") is pure cost-benefit analysis: What is the potential payoff relative to the cost? More specifically, make sure you fully understand all the elements of both sides of the comparison. What are all the costs of pursuing whatever scheme has been presented to you, or you have dreamed up? Considering the long-shot nature of most GRQS you or I have ever heard of, that means the cost must be *very* low for the attempt to be considered at all. If the scheme costs *any* money, it probably is not worth it. If it costs any money whatsoever and is something presented to you by another person, it is probably a scam. This is also probably not news to you.

To be considered, too, is the cost of your time and effort. If you weren't going to be doing anything worthwhile anyway, this factor vanishes. But how often is that going to be true? Your time is always of value, isn't it?

Consideration of the benefit side, the payoff, may not be as straightforward as it first appears either. Not only must the *amount* of potential payoff be forecast, but its *likelihood* of occurrence must also be assessed. A very low or infinitesimal probability of a high payoff is still a low "expected" result, in the language of statisticians.

In addition to the monetary or economic value you are seeking through your GRQS, another benefit you receive is any enjoyment, entertainment, or fun you derive from the process of pursuing the scheme. Any labor or difficulty associated with the GRQS is part of the cost, but it is possible that the activity itself will produce some enjoyment. That has to be taken into account in the benefit side relative to the costs, as may be found in some of the following illustrations, again from my own experience primarily. (We're getting too serious here. It's time for another sideshow.)

GRQS #1: Cosmetics, Midgets, and Dare to Be Great. You've seen late-night TV infomercials. They pitch a variety of products and business opportunities. Some are fairly legitimate; many tend toward the shady side. One of the more questionable practices is the peddling of "pyramid" sales schemes, sometimes euphemistically called "multilevel" marketing. (When you hear the pitch-man claim that "it is taught at the Harvard Business School," he means descriptively, not *prescrip-*

tively. In other words, the practice might have been mentioned or described by a Harvard professor in class, as I describe it to you here, but certainly not *recommended* as a business method.) What the multi-level pyramid refers to, essentially, is the selling of distributorships as well as products, making your customer also a dealer, and receiving, presumably, commissions on all products sold by your dealers, not only on the merchandise you sell. Then, as your dealers sell dealerships (from which you are also supposed to receive commissions), the pyramid is built up. It breaks down in practice, however, because after a few levels in the chain are constructed, almost all the people on earth would have to be in the pyramid to avoid the problem of all existing members, even those at a single level in the structure, competing destructively with one another for product and distributorship sales.

One of the pyramid scheme pioneers in the early 1970s was a huckster named Glenn W. Turner, who was pretty notorious at the time. His most well-known pyramid organizations were *Koscot Interplanetary*, which marketed cosmetics (and the related distributorships), and *Dare to Be Great*, which pushed a self-development course. Turner was a flamboyant character, to say the least, who traveled around the country in his Lear jet with an entourage of showgirls and midgets. He boasted of his wealth, his reconstructed harelip, and his poor background.

Did I invest in one of Glenn Turner's pyramids? Was that the scheme? Of course not. In 1972, I think it was, while I was still a university student, Glenn Turner visited our business school as an invited speaker. He attracted a large audience including my friend Nasty John, whom I've already introduced to you, and me. Turner put on quite a show, on stage with his entourage, energetically describing his modest beginnings in door-to-door sales, his controversial image, and his scrapes with the law because of fraud accusations (while proclaiming his innocence). As one of my profs said to me later, "This guy is a charlatan, but he had that audience mesmerized. The only one who had the nerve to challenge him was you, John." This is what I said to Glenn W. Turner during his question-and-answer session on that occasion, verbatim:

Mr. Turner, you've just told us you are such a good sales-man that you could make a living selling horse manure door-to-door. Well, everything I've heard about your cosmetics products suggests that is exactly what you *are* doing.

That brought the house down. Some of our older faculty, who were there at the time, still talk about it. But Glenn Turner and I weren't finished.

After his presentation, John and I, not to miss an opportunity, approached Mr. Turner and asked him to give us $50,000 so we could start a business—hoping he would empathize with our audacity. (I'm sure buying a bar or something like that, which I did later in life, is what we had in mind.) He turned us down, but did impart some worthwhile advice, to my surprise. Without missing a beat, he said if he were to give us that money, it would make us weak, but if we got that money on our own, we would be stronger as a result. I believe there is much truth in that comment.

The "get rich quick" aspect of this was the attempt to get a free $50,000 out of someone who had it, and just might have been eccentric enough to part with it. (In today's dollars, that $50,000 is the equivalent of about $150,000.) Was our effort a failure, as it would seem on the surface? Hardly. Let's add up the score. Cost: negligible, virtually nothing, only a few moments of our time. Benefits: actual payoff of zero, potential payoff of $50,000. Supplementary benefits: unexpect-edly good advice and the corollary payoff of some amusing interaction with the one and only Glenn Turner, which provides me with a colorful anecdote to this day. That scheme was a winner, but we are looking for a little bigger payoff, aren't we? How about one worth $745,000?

GRQS #2: The $745,000 "Hammer." This has nothing to do with wasteful federal government procurement.

Before Barry Bonds there was Hank Aaron. In 1975 the great baseball slugger Hank Aaron was concluding his fabulous career, in which he became the leading home run hitter of all time. Toward the end of that 1975 season it had become pretty apparent that "Hammerin' Hank" would be retiring, which led me to wonder when, and where, he would hit his final home run. Considering all the attention that had been given to his 715th homer, which broke Babe Ruth's career record, and the long-standing significance of the number 714 in baseball lore, it occurred to me that Mr. Aaron's final career home run might realistically come to be regarded as the greatest milestone in major league baseball history—and the ball he would hit it with might become the supreme sports artifact ever, and an object of great commercial value! That was it. That was my scheme. "I'm going to catch Hank Aaron's last home run ball, and it's going to make me rich," I thought. The prospect of so doing was not as far-fetched, not as "high off the wall" (pardon the puns), as you might think. Don't read my lips, read my plan:

First, I speculated that Aaron's last homer would not occur in the final series of the year, in his home park (he was with the Milwaukee Brewers then). That would have been too perfect. I played the hunch that the "shot heard 'round the world" would happen during his team's next-to-last series, a three game set in Cleveland with the Indians, and made plans to attend those games. What kind of probabilities are we dealing with? Aaron's home run ratio for that season was ten (hit as of that point) over approximately 150 *team* games, the relevant basis as opposed to the number he played in personally. In other words, at one home run every 15 games, the odds were 15-to-one, against, that "The Hammer" would homer in any game his team played, i.e., 150/10. Over a three game series, therefore, it was only about a *five-to-one* chance I was taking, statistically, that Hank Aaron would hit a home run.[1] How could I assume I would be the one to catch the home run ball?—because I was prepared to do *anything* to get it. Given a Hank Aaron home run during that series in Cleveland, the odds were about 100% that I would come away with it.

But what if Hank does hammer one in Cleveland, and then homers again in the next series— without me being there? We have to allow for that possibility, which slightly increases the odds. How so? There are four relevant combinations to consider:

1. Homers in Cleveland, does not in final series—my success formula.
2. Homers in Cleveland, does again in final series— foiled!
3. Does not homer in Cleveland, does not in final series.
4. Does not homer in Cleveland, does in final series.

The latter two are already accounted for by the original 5-1 odds, so the (lesser) statistical chance of #2 occurring, relative to #1, makes my scheme closer to a *seven-to-one* shot. A lucky number, I was hoping, and not bad odds at all considering the payoff. But what *was* the prospective payoff?

As soon as I got this idea, I called my friend Nasty John (him, again) in Cleveland, at 2 A.M., to inform him how we were going to get rich by catching Hank Aaron's last home run. First, he would get tickets for the targeted series with the Brewers. (No problem. The "Tribe" had a terrible team and demand for tickets was very low— which made for less competition for us.) We would sit in the left field grandstand, to be in ideal position to retrieve any home run balls of right-handed "pull" hitters like Aaron. (Once there, I realized I was correct to have estimated a conditional 100% likelihood of getting *the* home run ball. Very few other spectators were in that area of Cleveland Municipal Stadium, or any other area, though a few more would gravitate out there whenever Mr. Aaron came to bat.) Upon obtaining, by *any* means necessary, a Hank Aaron home run ball, our procedure was to be this:

First, we secure witnesses, especially stadium personnel such as ushers, including names and addresses if possible. Then we ask to be taken to the team office and press box. Once there, we announce to the baseball world (1) what we have in our possession, (2) its likely historical significance (i.e., the ultimate in sports memorabilia), (3) that the ball is for sale, actually being held for ransom, (4) that the price for (what would have been) home run #745 is *$745,000*, a fitting sum for such a unique trophy, and (5) our sincere hope that the Brewers organization, Major League Baseball, some rich philanthropist, or a consortium of

Mr. Aaron's endorsement sponsors would raise the money to ensure that the greatest of all sports artifacts would find its rightful place in its hitter's possession, or perhaps in the Hall of Fame. In the meantime, we would put the souvenir in a jointly-held safe deposit box.

The initial public reaction to all of that surely would have been scoffing resistance, possibly revulsion, disbelief, noncompliance, and widespread rooting for Hank Aaron to hit another home run. Maybe we would have waited forever for the "ransom" to be paid, but maybe not. A comparable amount was paid for Barry Bonds's record-breaker.

How did this scheme turn out? As you've probably gathered, Hank Aaron did not cooperate, at any phase of the plan. Not only did "The Hammer" not homer for us while we attended the Cleveland-Milwaukee series in late September of 1975, he did hit one in the next series in Milwaukee, and then he decided to play *another year*, during which he homered ten more times. Whoever caught Aaron home run #755 needs to read this.

So this unusual "get rich quick" scheme is to be considered a miserable failure? Technically, perhaps, but for the price of a trip to Cleveland I got: a trip to beautiful and exotic Cleveland. I got to experience a major league ballpark that I never would have set foot in otherwise. I did witness home runs by the immortal George Hendrick and Charlie Spikes. Of course, I still get grief from John for that particular brainstorm. For a chance at $745,000 (over $2 million in current dollars), though, not a bad risk. It was fun. I just have always made sure I don't tell many people about that one— until now.

GRQS #3: $610,000! I could cry. When people ask me what's the most money I've ever lost, I just tell them $610,000. Here's how it happened.

As mentioned briefly in an earlier chapter, my grandfather and step-grandmother were pretty well-off by the standards of the day. It was always anticipated that my mother would someday inherit a substantial sum from them. (As an only child, I would be the ultimate heir—though certainly not a prospect I ever looked forward to.) My grandfather had intended to adjust their estate plan to ensure this, but it did not seem a crucial matter. His wife was rather sickly and it seemed likely he would survive her. (Believe me, these morbid considerations were never in the forefront of our consciousness at the time.) But then the unexpected happened, and my grandfather passed away first. Two years later, when his wife died, almost the entire estate, $610,000 worth (about $1.8 million in today's dollars), went to her nephew— a nice enough fellow, but not as nice or deserving as my mother, who had waited on her step-mother hand and foot as though a blood relative.

It was a completely innocent oversight by my grandfather, who was universally known as one of the finest human beings you could ever meet, but it dramatizes the necessity of attentive estate planning. Though an unpleasant chore, don't let it slip, don't put it off, face up to it, and the sooner the better. The younger you are when you do it, the less morbid it will seem. I had my will done when I was 32, for *free*, of course. Two lawyer friends of mine, a husband and wife team, did my will as a favor, although I did buy them a case of beer out of grati-tude, enduring gratitude. With Notre Dame as my heir, it is especially comforting to know that I will be immortal, via an endowed scholarship fund supporting needy and deserving business students in the name of my parents and me, perpetually. I'll be grinning in my grave next to that 16th fairway. If that's what does it for me, in eternity, something else entirely will be your motive for estate planning, such as averting the kind of error that damaged my mother. Either way, don't allow it to fall between the cracks. So the moral is: estate planning— YES. It is especially appropriate now that you will be accumulating an estate.

Back to the GRQS narrative: A few years after being virtually stiffed by my step-grandmother's estate, I decided to make one bona fide at-tempt to rectify the injustice done my mother, low probability crusade as that might be. I visited the inheritor, the deceased step-grandmother's nephew (I don't think I've ever used that expression before), to appeal for some consideration to my mother, some financial consideration. I scheduled an appointment with him, at his farmhouse, to try to persuade him to cede a fair share of the estate proceeds to my mother. (He was already so rich he could have afforded to easily. Any amount would have assuaged my mother's hurt feelings.) I don't want to go into detail, but I used every type of appeal I could recall from communication theory—empathy, sympathy, equity, justice, self-interest, everything. I never was much of a salesman and was true to form on that occasion, as anticipated, but I had to try. I could not passively allow such an injustice without making some effort to correct it.

Another failure? I don't think so. The cost: only a little time and effort, and the discomfort of being in the role of salesman and supplicant—a small price to pay on behalf of my mother. Potential payoff: unknown. Actual payoff: (1) zippo, monetarily; (2) peace of mind from knowing I did my best, and left no stone unturned. My conscience is clear. (3) Though not a direct benefit of the GRQS endeavor, I really believe I am *better off* because our family was deprived of a substantial inheritance. As Glenn Turner said, it would have made me weak. I truly believe I appreciate the value of money more as a result of that loss, and this attitude, as should have been demonstrated by now, is invaluable.

One last thing: The punch line didn't occur for over 15 years, when there was an item about the inheritor-nephew-farmer in the local paper. The school board and city government had offered him $800,000 for a *piece* of his farmland, but he turned them down. He was quoted as saying he "didn't need the money." I let him know how I felt about that, in view of his lack of consideration 15 years earlier. A tightwad never forgets.

GRQS #4: The Textbook Approach (which means it works in the real world, too). Instead of another anecdote, you will now receive what marketing students get, which is nothing less than *how to get people to give you their money*. Would that be a useful ability for you to have?

The first thing to recognize is . . . no, you tell me. What would induce you to give money to someone else? After what we've covered, it would probably take quite a bit. That's the answer. If *A* wants to get money from *B*, *A* must do something *for B*. *A* must offer something that will *satisfy B*, something of real *value* to *B*. In other words, *A* must provide a good *product* for *B*. So the question is, how do you know what a good product is? How do you come up with, or create, a good product—for which people actually will part with their money?

The starting point for developing a good product is recognition of a customer or market *need that is unfulfilled*. Then, of course, you have to have, or be able to develop, the capability to fulfill it. That is the essence of marketing and the essence of free-market commerce. Identify a customer need or want, and satisfy it. Find an uncovered hole in the market, and fill it.

How do you discover a market need yearning to be satisfied? In business, it is difficult enough, but there are ways. Businesses are constantly monitoring the market environment through research for this very purpose, but they do not overlook the straightforward approach of *asking people*. Marketers continually are interviewing their salespeople, engineers, distributors, advertising agencies, and customers themselves about needs that are not being met, or are not met very well. In other words, they are searching for product deficiency or product void, which means an opportunity to fix it or fill it by providing a satisfactory product.

With the individual, something similar can be done. You do not have a research staff, so you can begin by studying the consumer directly. That consumer is you. Be alert to product deficiencies, product failures (among the very few product categories you still buy, as you are getting rich by not spending much money), or product absence, i.e., products that don't exist, but should. Also pay attention to expressions of consumer discontent by friends and family members. This is step number one.

But how do you *really* discover a good product idea that will satisfy a need? Forget the textbook gobbledegook, you say; how does one really identify something that will sell? When I let my hair down with my students, I tell them that one sure-fire good product is anything that eliminates a *pain in the ass*— anything that relieves a nuisance, resolves an inconvenience, removes an annoyance, or solves a problem. Products are problem-solvers, fundamentally. As fictional secret agent *007*, James Bond, once said, "The termination of pain is far more satisfying than the most intense pleasure," and he was in a position to know about both. When trying to come up with new products, therefore, don't just think in terms of converting a neutral situation to positive for a customer, also try to think of opportunities to *convert a negative situation to neutral.* That is a service, and benefit, that people will pay good money for.

So let's say you do get an idea for a new product, and you want to become an entrepreneur. You want to start a business to produce and market that product. Or let's say it's not a new product at all, just a different version of someone else's product which doesn't seem to be satisfying customers very well, in your opinion. Or you want to provide a service, and you think you can compete with others in that kind of business. Let's say you want to become a retailer, a wholesaler, or even open a barber shop. *And*, since you've been on the program to get rich without making very much money for awhile, you have enough capital to take the plunge. Should you risk it?

The next thing you have to do is critically evaluate your product or business idea. Everybody thinks their idea is great initially, but the overwhelming majority of new products and new businesses fail. Use your own judgment, trying to think of everything that could possibly go wrong. Are the problems correctable and the weaknesses manageable? Run the idea by friends. Seek advice from others, especially experts who might actually know something helpful. (As we go through this, try to think in terms of a real product or business idea you have had. Rather than just my abstractions and generalities, try to see how this information would apply to a real situation. I will have a real-life example for you soon.)

The most important part of this critical appraisal in practical terms, and usually the most difficult, is developing some kind of a forecast of the profit potential of the business idea. One would not want to go forward any further with a project unless there is a reasonable and measurable opportunity for profit. You need some idea of the demand or potential sales for the product, along with knowledge of costs, therefore. Again, businesses such as large corporations have a research infrastructure, including sophisticated technology, to perform this function. Small mom-and-pop type operations either "fly by the seat of the pants" on this or seek help from a consultant. For the budding entrepreneur, the most feasible approaches to getting a handle on sales potential might involve (a) the substitute approach— if the product is intended to replace something else, how much does that "something else" sell? or (b) asking as many people as possible whether they would buy the product, or whether they would buy services from your business (e.g., your store or barber shop), and *how much* they would buy per month or year; then computing a per customer average across all those polled, and multiplying by the estimated number of customers in the market, for an overall estimate of market potential.

For cost estimates, production and marketing costs and everything else, start Googling the web or see a public accountant.

Naturally, demand and profit forecasting for a new product or business, if done properly, is a very detailed, quantitative, technical, and complicated undertaking, far beyond the capabilities of most individuals. As long as you understand what you *need* to do in this regard, though, if you ever do become an entrepreneur and go into business for yourself, with real money on the line, you will find a way to at least rough out an estimate.

One final task in developing a new product is creating a model or prototype. You have to hire someone to produce a few samples, if it is a physical product (and this escalates your investment, underscoring the importance of the previous phase). In the case of a service this would involve a practice session, dry-run, or dress rehearsal of providing the service. The main purpose here is to ensure that the product (or the service) performs as intended, does what it is supposed to do. This is a chance to work out the "bugs."

After all this, if *producing* (or hiring out production of, rather than wholesaling or retailing) a product, you need to think about setting up a *distribution channel*. For most new businesses, first consider mail-order or internet sales, or agents known as "manufacturers' reps." You also would need to set the *price* and develop a *promotion* strategy. Naturally, I cannot give you a complete course in marketing here. That would take another book and at least several months— just for an introductory course. The preceding outline, however, provides you a rough summary of the *kinds* of things you would need to attend to if you ever intend to start a business. Cover all these bases, and it will point you in the direction of having the best chance of actually making money. Don't forget, the starting point is recognizing a need.

For the record, I do recommend a university business education if you wish to go into business. That should be seen as a less-than-radical statement.

GRQS #4a: The Textbook. Naturally, I believe in everything I just gave you. If and when I wish to make money (without working for it through employment), I will apply the principles of #4 above. In fact, I feel the urge coming on right now. Let's go through the procedure and see if we come up with something.

What in the world could I possibly do for other people to make them want to give me money? It certainly wouldn't be manual labor, because I don't believe in it (for myself). So it will have to be some kind of intellectual service, some knowledge-based product. But what? What do I *know* that could conceivably be of value to someone else? (The marketing information I give my students is valuable to them— they just don't realize it.) I've got it! One thing and one thing only: If there's one thing I know that would be useful and valuable to others, it is the knowledge of *how to get rich without making very much money.* I know the subject because I've seen it done and I've done it. Transmitting that knowledge to others is a service large numbers of people surely would pay good money for because it does not appear as though the general public shares that knowledge, based on available evidence on saving rates. So there would seem to be a ready market opportunity for me, a common need that I can meet. That was step one, identifying the opportunity to do a book on getting rich without even having to make much money.

Is there anything wrong with this idea? What about competition? What if someone else comes out with the same kind of product? No problem. I haven't checked and I'm not going to, but no one else could possibly produce the *type* of product, or book, that I have in mind. Even if something else were published on the same general theme, I doubt if any other author would come up with my special slant: the *lighter side* of getting rich, how you can do it and have fun, without even making very much money. I will have a monopoly, therefore.

How large would the market be for a book like this? You tell me. How many people would *not* benefit from the ability this book attempts to provide? That would only be the very rich, so the potential market would be gigantic. The "seat of the pants" method of demand estimation, i.e., guessing, is adequate in this case because the answer is so self-evident.

What about creating a sample or prototype of my product? The closest things to that in this instance are the "mock-up" versions, i.e., the outline I worked from and the synopsis submitted to the publisher. Distribution, pricing, and promotion of the *final* product are the domain of the publisher, but from the perspective of my rough manuscript, the key variables were (1) creating an attractive submission package, including cover letter (promotion), and (2) making it as easy and convenient as possible for a publisher's reviewer to read the manuscript (low price, in effect).

I applied the textbook approach to creating and marketing the product you hold in your hand, in essence a "textbook" of how to get rich without making very much money. I just hope it doesn't read too much like a textbook.

My motivation all along has been self-interest or profit? Yes and no. Like any enlightened producer/marketer of goods and services, I have had dual motives. I realize that if I wish to receive money from others, I must do something for them. From all my years of studying the subject of marketing, I also understand that the *best* way to make money is to offer a product that genuinely provides a benefit and satisfies a need, one that really delivers what it promises, rather than manipulating customers into buying a bad product. (This explains preceding case #3, in which the product I attempted to sell was inherently unattractive.) The author of this volume has been uncompromisingly devoted to the reader's success at getting rich, therefore, because that is in the author's own interest. This convergence of interests is the way capitalism works. The best way to ensure your self-interest in free commerce is to ensure the customer's satisfaction, and that means providing a high-quality product. Exceptions to this principle are rare, if you really think about it, and require unusual circumstances. Gaining profit, or self-interest, *through the means* of genuinely satisfying your customer is the very definition of marketing, in fact, contrary to what you might have thought. (This reality is also part of the reason the former Eastern Bloc countries have had such a difficult time converting to capitalist prosperity. The people of those countries had been brainwashed, over many decades, into believing that capitalism is a matter of ruthless swindling or cheating of customers— so when they try it, it doesn't work very well. In fact, the opposite is the rule.)

There probably are few among us who have not had a "get rich quick" idea at one time or another. Like anything else, cost-benefit analysis can be helpful in evaluating whether to proceed with a venture. Here that involves assessment of the potential and expected payoffs. No matter how high the potential payoff, if the probability is miniscule, the prospect may not be worth the effort and cost. If the cost in time, effort, and dollars is very low, however, even a lower or more remote payoff may be a sensible risk. Higher cost (ad)ventures would obviously necessitate a greater payoff or a higher likelihood of its fulfillment. And when comparing costs and benefits, don't neglect to factor in whatever *fun* you are going to have while pursuing your "get rich" dream. Though my GRQS #1-3 were all technical failures, I record them as authentic successes when adding that extra dimension to my computation of payout. So if a scheme appears to meet the criteria we have laid out (or yours which may well be more sophisticated than mine), why not? Take a chance. If it doesn't work out, you'll still be getting rich the other way!

Take a Chance, He Says?

What about the more traditional approaches to "getting rich quick," such as the lottery, sweepstakes, and other forms of gambling? The lottery is a bad bet. Typically it pays out about 50 cents on the dollar, closer to 35 cents after taxes. The lottery is a matter of heads, you win 35 cents, tails, you lose a dollar.[2]

Sweepstakes, like the thing you receive in the mail from Ed Mc-Mahon, aren't much better. At least your entry fee is only the cost of a 42 cent stamp. Say the odds of winning a meaningful prize of a million dollars or so in a particular sweepstakes are about ten million-to-one, which would be fairly representative of ones I've seen. A million dollars divided by ten million is 10 cents. That is your payoff's "expected value," as they say in the field of academic statistics. Even at a cost of 42 cents, your *net* expected value is negative. Of course, if you enter sweepstakes regularly, the probability is cumulative. Enter a hundred of the kind just described, and the odds of winning a million bucks are only about 100,000-to-one (expected value of $10). Enter a thousand and your chances have improved to 10,000-to-one (E.V. = $100).[3] But your cumulative postage costs would then be $42 and $420, respectively, so the net expectation would still be a loser.

All this does not necessarily mean that it is irrational to play sweepstakes or the lottery. You may be perfectly willing, sensibly, to accept those small losses, in absolute terms, over a long period of time. As much as we would regret a negative net expected value of $320 over a thousand plays, that's not much in comparison with the *potential* payoff, also including the possible enjoyment of playing. We may choose to play even with such accurate foreknowledge of the adverse expected outcome. Economists call this tendency "risk preference," and it is perfectly rational. Just don't ever imagine that such gaming is anything but a losing bet, in an expected value sense. Maybe you can find a sweepstakes that offers better odds of a higher payout, producing a positive expected value, but don't count on it.

Concerning other conventional forms of wagering, e.g., casino gambling, I can't tell you much. The first time I ever went to Las Vegas (on a free trip, naturally) I was bored to death for my first three or four days there because I don't care for casino gambling. I was bored, at least, until I learned to appreciate just soaking up all the opulence and decadence. I have thoroughly enjoyed inhaling the Vegas atmosphere on my subsequent four or five free trips there, without gambling much and without losing anything. That is a payout ratio of *infinity*: some considerable enjoyment at no cost. The "mob" certainly did one thing right.

What little information I can impart to you on the subject of gambling (*legal* wagering, of course) is of great importance, however. I may not know from *diddly squat* about casino-type gambling, as suggested. I am aware that it is possible to win at the game of blackjack, as the so-called "card counters" do, but I do not know how it is done because I have never studied it. Friends inform me that one can win regularly at craps, based on a slight edge gained over others playing, but I do not know that to be true. What I do know something about is horse racing, and horse playing. I can tell you that it is possible to win regularly at thoroughbred pari-mutuel wagering. ("Pari-mutuel" means you are playing against the other bettors, not the "house.") I can *show* you how to win at the race track. The most amazing thing of all about this, I believe, is that if I show you how to win money consistently at the race track, you will not want to do it.

I studied thoroughbred handicapping (which just means "method of analyzing horse race entrants") primarily for one reason. Every spring, like clockwork in early May— the time of the Kentucky Derby—

it seems almost everyone becomes an instant horse racing expert. Everybody and their brother have a pick for the Derby, even though they know absolutely nothing of what they are talking about. I decided I wanted to be different from those people. I wanted to be one of the few who actually do know something about horse racing. So I studied the leading textbook on thoroughbred handicapping, Ainslie's *The Compleat Horseplayer*, and distilled its content.[4] The basic method of picking horses that the best professional horse players use is a step-by-step elimination process incorporating these 11 elements: distance, form, weight, class, sex, consistency, jockey, pace rating (a variation of the concept of speed), class rating, miscellaneous factors, and paddock appearance. The complication is that each of these factors involves several conditions or tests. (The "miscellaneous" category alone includes 27 different criteria to apply.) Here's an example of the "distance" analysis:

Three-year-olds and up, claiming races up to and including a mile:

1. Must have finished at least 4th in a straight claiming race at today's distance at a major track. Until June 30, a 3-year-old is acceptable if it has finished at least 6th, within two lengths of winner, in a race of higher claiming price than today's. Also acceptable if it has won a maiden-special weights or maiden claimer of a price at least 25% higher than today's claiming price.

2. Must have run today's distance on today's track (or circuit), earning a speed rating of at least 80 while finishing no worse than 5½ lengths behind the winner. If today's claiming price is $4000 or less, accept speed rating of 78 provided no rival shows 81 or better.

3. The good race on this track or on this circuit should have occurred this season.

Allowance and handicap races at a mile or less: Same general rules apply except when some contenders have achieved speed ratings in 90s, eliminate anything unable to get above 85.

Races at 11/16 mile or farther, same general rules except: claiming races—speed rating of 75 needed to qualify; allowance & handicap races—at least an 80; claiming prices of $4000 or less—accept a 69.

Races at 11/8 mile or longer: Past-performance record must show either that horse has won or has finished in the money while gaining ground in the stretch in a race of the prescribed distance.

Then, on and on like that, or worse, through the 11 categories of analysis. (My editor wouldn't allow any more of this tedious material to be printed here.)

There you have it. The people who make their living by playing the horses do it like this. How do you like it?

What's the matter? Go ahead and use the system to make money. Go right ahead. It really works. What's the problem? Don't you like it?

The problem, obviously, is that the method of analysis outlined here is very laborious, to say the least. There is hardly enough time to apply the method during the 20 minutes or so between races in a daily program of racing, so you have to get a copy of the *Racing Form* in advance and then spend several hours doing the analytical homework before going to the track or the off-track betting parlor. It is hard work. It is very hard work. It is mentally-taxing labor. After a program of eight to ten races, I am rather exhausted (and I didn't even have to run around the track). The professional horseplayers can do it more easily, because they have internalized the method and it is second nature to them. They can look at a page from the *Racing Form* and analyze a race practically at a glance, but only after many years of practice.

These veteran horseplayers also can do this well enough to earn a living from their craft. But most of them *barely* make a living. They do not get rich from this knowledge. The best professional thorough-bred handicappers, for the most part, barely eke out a living from their winnings. To actually earn a living from playing the horses is quite an achievement, I believe, but is it an attractive career and way of life? Might such people deserve their stereotyped image of sleazy or low-life? In view of (1) the effort involved in learning and applying the standard method, (2) the risk (a player might have to ride out a dry spell of several weeks with no income), and (3) the moderate payoff, at best, would the profession of horseplaying be an efficient economic endeavor for you, or anyone? It might be only if great enjoyment were derived from the process itself (i.e., qualitatively enhancing the payoff side), but you're in this to get rich, aren't you? You probably can't get rich from this method. I've given you an easier way than that to get rich!

Another lesson: How dull was this section on horse racing? Pretty boring, wasn't it? Well then, how would you like to have to make your living—a modest living at that—by applying yourself to such deadly dull subject matter?

Yet for anyone who wishes to earn a living, barely, instead of getting rich, and wishes to do it through very hard work, you may begin by studying and digesting the Ainslie book as I did, which is cited for that contingency. See you at the track, though I'll only be there once or twice a year. I can't take too much hard labor.

Chapter 8

Finally, A Sure Thing *OR* Now That You're Beginning to Get Rich, What Do You Do With All That Money?

You should soon be saving more than you ever thought possible. Unfortunately, money does not come with instructions. What should you be doing with your money? How should you invest it? To these questions, there are some definite and reliable answers. Investing money is a much more straightforward undertaking than the general public realizes. Proper investing, through proven methods, is at hand. It offers much better odds than Las Vegas, the lottery, or sweepstakes, and demands much less effort than picking horses. In fact, it involves no effort whatsoever. First, some reminders:

Take What the Boss and the Government Give You

Make sure you participate in any pension plan your employer makes available, such as the "401(k)" deal. Generally employers match employee contributions, if not dollar for dollar they may at least add 25 cents or 50 cents on top of each dollar the employee contributes. This is a rare case in which *free money* is available.[1] A 50-cent-on-the-dollar employer augmentation is an instant return of 50% on your money. A dollar-for-dollar addition is a return of 100%, instantly! Be sure, as well, to have your own contributions made through salary "reduction" rather than straight deduction, because that will also reduce your taxable income.

You have probably heard what a good deal an "individual retirement account" (IRA) is. You heard right. The special benefits of an IRA are: (1) The income earned is tax-*deferred* until withdrawal (which begins between the ages of 59 1/2 and 70, as you may choose). (2) For many people, especially those with lower incomes, IRA contributions are tax-*deductible* up to the $5000 annual maximum investment. (3) Now, the newer Roth IRA, though non-deductible, allows tax-*exempt* earnings and withdrawals, without some restrictions of other IRAs. Anyone aged 70 or under who earns employment income may make annual contributions to a traditional IRA. The contributions are fully deductible if (a) neither you nor your spouse participate in an employer-sponsored retirement plan, or (b) you have adjusted gross income (as of tax year 2008) of no more than $85,000 ($53,000 for individuals). If income is greater than that limitation, IRA contributions are partially deductible, until phased out at $105,000/$63,000 of married/single adjusted income. About 80% of U.S. households are eligible for full or partial IRA deductions. Even if your contribution is not deductible, an additional benefit is that its eventual distributions are tax-*free* (since they've already been taxed once), and are not subject to the 10% penalty for early withdrawal, which applies to deductible IRAs. (Because of the increased complexity since the advent of the Roth IRA, you should consult a good reference, such as brochures available from any mutual fund company, before making an IRA investment.) Table 8-1 shows the tremendous advantage of the opportunity to build wealth in a traditional tax-deferred IRA, compared with a taxable investment.[2] For example, an IRA held for 35 years, with $2000 annual contributions, is worth $307,071 more than the corresponding taxable account because of tax-deferred compounding—apart from any available tax-*deduction* benefits!

TABLE 8-1

Example of IRA Tax-Deferral Benefit

Value at Age 65 @ 10% Annual Return[a]

Age to Start	Total Contributions	Taxable Investment	IRA
30	$70,000	$289,183	$596,254
35	60,000	198,360	361,887
40	50,000	133,301	216,364
45	40,000	86,697	126,005
50	30,000	53,314	69,899

[a]Assumes $2000 contributions made at beginning of each year and 31% tax bracket.

When explaining in Chapter 3 why you should be afraid *not* to start saving, examples of garden-variety IRAs were supplied. A more dramatic example is this one: Person A starts a traditional IRA at age *21*, depositing $2000 a year for *six years*. Person B begins an IRA at *27* and contributes $2000 annually *until age 65*. Person C establishes an IRA at *21* years of age and inputs the $2000 annually *until age 65*. *C* will be the winner, of course, but what are the comparative totals? Assuming a 12% annual compounded return (less conservative but probably more realistic than the earlier 10% assumption), the scoreboard looks like Table 8-2, revealing starkly the advantage of getting an early start on a saving program. Even though *B* contributes $66,000 and 33 years more than *A*, their end values are about the same.[3]

TABLE 8-2

Three IRA Plans

	Total Contributions	Value at Age 65
Person A	$12,000 (6 yrs.)	$1,348,440
Person B	78,000 (39 yrs.)	1,363,780
Person C	90,000 (45 yrs.)	2,714,460

Now that you are going to have money to invest, you should give serious consideration to the realities, lessons, and implications of these tables. After setting aside emergency cash equal to about three to six months' income, one of your first investment actions should probably be to inaugurate an IRA, whether you qualify for deductibility or not. It is almost always a great deal. And make your annual contribution as close to the very beginning of the calendar year as possible, so you reap the benefit of tax-deferred compounding of your dollars for the maximum amount of time.

Take What the Markets Give You

Whether you are investing through an IRA, or investing your non-IRA funds, where should you put the money? Should you invest in stocks, bonds, or what? (The above examples assume stock market-type returns.) Again, the answer may be more definite than many realize, as revealed in the following information.

If you had invested $1000 in U.S. Treasury bills (short-term promissory obligations of the Federal government) in 1950, compounding by rolling the investment over at each maturity, by the year 2000 your investment would have been worth $12,300. If you had originally put your money in long-term Treasury bonds on the same terms, the Y2000 value would be up to $15,020. Had you invested the $1000 in the stock market, buying a cross-section of 500 of the largest New York Stock Exchange companies (known as the "Standard & Poor's 500"), compounding by reinvesting all dividends, 50 years later you would have had a total of $510,160.[4]

The average annual return you get from common stocks, based on 1926-2008 S&P 500 results, is 10.3%. (It is around 12% in the more recent decades.) Compare that with a 5.5% historical return for long-term corporate bonds over the same period, and 3.5% available from Treasury bills.[5]

The *cumulative* return from Treasury bills for the 27-year period between 1973 and 2000 was 505%. Treasury bonds yielded a return of 877%, cumulatively, over the same two-plus decades. U.S. common stocks, as represented by the S&P 500 again, generated a cumulative return of *3254%* for the 27 years ending in 2000.[6]

The results are in. No other category of financial asset can match the long-term performance of common stocks, or even come close. The implication is clear. If you have a long-range time horizon, say at least five years or more, the prudent asset class to choose for your investment dollars is common stocks. Stocks certainly fluctuate more than bonds, Treasury bills, or money market funds over the short-term, as we have recently seen, so they are not the right vehicle for money you will need next month or maybe even next year, but you can't beat them over long periods— based on all available evidence over the decades, though no one can predict the future with certainty. The reason stocks are considered the *prudent* long-run investment vehicle is that you risk forfeiting so much potential gain if you choose the less volatile, more conservative, asset categories like bonds, bank certificates of deposit (CD's), Treasury bills, or money market funds. (Money market funds are mutual funds that invest in short-term promissory notes of corporations or governments, such as municipalities.)

But *how* does one invest in stocks? Do you buy individual stocks through the advice of a stockbroker? Do you just invest through mutual funds? (A mutual fund is an organization that pools the money of many investors to buy financial assets such as stocks, bonds, or money market instruments. Some private companies put money into factories, which they operate; they are called *manufacturers*. Some companies put their money into stores, which they operate; they are called *retailers*. Companies that invest in other companies' stock are called stock *mutual funds* or investment companies.) Or should you hang the newspaper stock listings on the wall and throw darts at it? What is the best way to pick stocks? How do you get into the stock market? What is the most profitable way to play the market? There is a very definite answer to these questions, and that answer may *really* surprise you.

The Right Answer

You would like to know the most profitable stock market investment strategy. Naturally, a question of such magnitude, with such colossal financial implications, has already been investigated thoroughly. Numerous business researchers and economists, in the private sector and at major universities, have done scientific studies on that very issue over the last three or four decades. The results have been consistent, in fact overwhelming. The answer is known, as well as anything can be known. The answer is: No investment strategy has ever been found that outperforms the simplest possible approach of *buying and holding a market portfolio*. ("Market" portfolio means a diversified cross-section of the stock market, e.g., the S&P 500, or a *randomly selected* stock portfolio. A random selection of stocks would be equivalent to the market portfolio, if a large enough number is selected at random.)

No alternative strategy has been found to match or exceed the returns offered by just buying and holding a diversified portfolio of stocks. No other trading strategy such as attempting to buy low and sell high, or trying to time the market, or forecasting turns in the market or the economy, or anything, has bettered the simple buy-and-hold approach. Another way of expressing this, based on evidence, is: Of all the professional stock pickers and money managers at investment companies, mutual funds, and brokerage houses, the number who outperform the market, i.e., the *average* of the S&P 500, is *fewer than would occur by random chance*. In other words, if the entire investment community abandoned their methods and instead made stock selections by *throwing darts blindfolded* at the newspaper listings (or by hiring chimpanzees to do the same), their performance, collectively, would be better than it actually is. If you were to buy stocks at random by throwing darts, there is a chance—random chance—that you would earn a return higher than the market average. The number of investment professionals who do beat the market is far lower than it would be if they *all* did it by random selection. Therefore, the rare exceptions who do outperform the market average cannot be attributed to anything but chance, i.e., dumb luck. Then those (e.g., mutual funds) that do exceed the market in a given period usually are underperformers in the next period. This is the explanation for apparent counterexamples you may think you are aware of. (Can we be sure there isn't one person or mutual fund somewhere that genuinely beats the market average by skill and judgment, rather than by chance? No, but as long as the number of investment managers who do is less than would happen by chance, it is pointless to make that assertion.)

The main reason for this phenomenon, the inability of judgmental or managed investment strategy to do as well as the most naïve buy-and-hold strategy, is what is known as *market efficiency*. The stock market has been found to be an efficient processor of all available information, so stock prices always contain and reflect that information. Market prices are fair, in other words. It is not possible to gain over the long-run, therefore, by selling one stock in order to buy another, i.e., "trading." If you purchase a favored stock because you think its price is too low relative to its value, and sell a non-favored one thinking its price is too high (overvalued), you are equally likely to lose as to gain, relative to your return had you *not* made the trade. The market's efficient pricing mechanism ensures this outcome—over the long run—because its fair prices, which fully reflect all available information, make it equally likely that any single stock issue will return more or less than the market. Also contributing to the investor's scientifically-demonstrated inability to beat the market average are *transaction costs*. If the probable future returns of two investments, a stock you favor and one you don't, are actually the same (i.e., each is equally likely to outperform the other) regardless of what the stock trader *thinks* at the time, selling one to buy another will be a losing event relative to "buy-and-hold" because of trading costs such as commissions and taxes.

Such a mountain of evidence supports this "efficient market" position that it is widely believed to be more evidence than supporting

169

anything in any other field of study, or at least any field having to do with human behavior.[7] Confirmed exceptions to this efficient market principle are rare: (1) genuine *insider information*, usually illegal to act upon, which is not publicly available and allows the possessor of it to gain an edge; (2) selected *inefficient markets*. Major exchange markets for stocks, bonds, commercial paper, commodities, and so forth are considered efficient, so all the above applies. Some markets, such as those for local residential real estate or collectibles, might not be efficient in the sense described, so "all bets are off" for them and there may exist opportunities for above-market returns.

What about that contest in *The Wall Street Journal* you may be familiar with, in which the professionals held a narrow lead over thrown-dart portfolios? Is this not contrary evidence? No. First, that contest's results were very short-term. Second, the real dart-selected portfolio over the long-term would be the *market average*, and the *Journal's* pros had only a slight edge over the market average. Finally, even that result is completely misleading because of one important factor the *Journal* did not take into account: transaction costs. Were the costs of switching from one professionally-selected stock portfolio to another in each period of the *Journal's* contest accounted for (results were tallied every six months), the stock-picking professionals' results would not have been superior to the market average—because they *can't* beat the market. Some of *The Wall Street Journal's* reporters are very confused.

But how does buy-and-hold strategy square with the "bear" market, or crash, of 2008? Wouldn't you as an investor have been better off if you had gotten out of stocks at their peak in 2007? Sure, but this does not invalidate the efficient market principle or buy-and-hold strategy. You see, investment decisions have to be made prospectively, not retrospectively. They have to be made in advance, not with the benefit of 20/20 hindsight. Of course, if you knew in advance that the stock market would tank, you could act on that knowledge. But no one knows in advance—although some think they do.

OK, what if you did predict the 2007-08 bear market, or the 1987 Black Monday crash, as some luckily did? (Underscore "luck.") Good for you, but no matter to this principle. How many times did you think the market would go down, or up, and turned out to be wrong?

The problem is that you, the investor, must guess right at least twice in a row. That is, you also have to be right about which alternative investment (bonds, gold, whatever) to buy, or when to get back into stocks. And you can't be right a high enough proportion of the time over the long term to offset the trading costs of commissions and taxes. And because of those costs, the return from such trading will be less than that delivered by random chance! Of course, historical results are not guaranteed to be duplicated in the future, but what I report to you is the best available evidence from the 1926-2008 period, along with the optimal strategy derived from it.

Again, you need not take my word for this. See anything in footnote #7, especially *A Random Walk Down Wall Street* by Malkiel, for a good explanation and summary of the evidence. Almost every finance prof in the world not only believes all this, but lives by it and profits from it.

Institutions in the investment community, i.e., mutual funds, brokerage houses, investment advisers, etc., also are well aware of this information on market efficiency and they can't stand it. Industry personnel are trained to argue against it. The firms issue counterpropaganda. Unfortunately for them, the implications of what has just been revealed to you are staggering, monumental, and could ultimately bring their industry down.

Implication #1. Since buy-and-hold has been proven to be the optimal strategy, once you have acquired a diversified portfolio, *it is always wrong to sell* an individual stock discretionarily thereafter. Anything other than holding everything indefinitely is irrational, therefore, subject to these exceptions: cash-need emergencies (an involuntary constraint), inside information (as just stipulated), and final liquidation of the portfolio (e.g., you're 65 or older and converting to fixed-income instruments, like bonds, which essentially is a matter of buying insurance). Even with the first and third exceptions, it is recognized that expected return still would be greater were buy-and-hold not violated.

Implication #2. The investment (i.e., financial advice or stock brokerage) industry is *largely* a fraud or hoax—or remarkably ignorant of scientific information about its own business. To the extent that the industry represents itself as being capable of providing advice, services, or a return that is any better than, or even equal to, that available from *hiring blindfolded chimpanzees to throw darts*, the investment industry's claims are demonstrably false.

Implication #3. If the investment industry's customers ever find out about this, a great many money managers and stockbrokers may be lynched. If and when investment customers realize that they can do as well or better by throwing darts blindfolded, it will be a major exposé, scandal, and maybe even a bloodbath. As one TV-savvy defense lawyer said during the O. J. trial, and as one Clinton mouthpiece said during impeachment, "This is a blockbuster. This is a bombshell." That imagery really does apply in this case.

The Ultimate Implication. As you can see, the way investing in the stock market really works is nothing at all like the general public thinks it works. It is much easier. It is a no-brainer. Since no other type of financial asset can compare with common stocks as far as long-run return goes, and since any strategy other than "buy and hold a diversified portfolio" has been proven a loser relative to that simple approach, the strategic implication is clear. The ideal strategy is to (1) have as much money in the stock market as you can comfortably afford *at all times*, and (2) buy a diversified portfolio and hold it through thick and thin, no matter what direction you think the market is headed. It has been proven that you can't guess *both* the ups and downs to be able to "buy low and sell high" often enough to offset transaction costs. Once you acquire a portfolio of stocks, just keep buying when you can and *never sell anything*, never sell any individual stock, until liquidation of the entire portfolio at age 65-70 or whenever.

How do you obtain a diversified or "market" portfolio? One of two ways: (1) Throw darts blindfolded—seriously, it has been verified that you can't beat it—as long as you have enough money to buy at least eight or ten issues (individual stocks) to achieve diversification; or (2) buy an "index" fund. An index fund is a mutual fund that just tries to mimic the overall market by owning a broad cross-section of issues, e.g., the S&P 500. The consensus *best* index funds, because they charge the lowest management fees, are offered by The Vanguard Group out of Valley Forge, PA, 1-800-662-7447. Ask for a prospectus on "stock index funds." You will be able to do all your business over the phone, through the mail, or on the web (www.vanguard.com).

The foregoing investment rules have been substantiated by voluminous evidence, so much that it's no contest. I didn't make this up. The case is closed— to the dismay of a predominantly fraudulent segment of the securities and investment industry, which would like you to believe that it can do something more for you than the blindfolded chimpanzees can. It can't. The Vanguard fund group candidly recognizes this, to your benefit. (And I trust you appreciate the irony and surrealistic incongruity. The one who reports this rather complex and esoteric information to you is the same one who saves store coupons, tried to catch Hank Aaron's last home run, wears his high school phys ed shirt, wrote the ad in Exhibit 2-1, and had braces put on his teeth to beat the military draft. But what difference does it make? Knowing how to get rich easily doesn't mean you can't have an interesting life. In fact, we've proven the two are perfectly compatible.)

Related Horror Stories

Speaking of candid, I hope you can learn from my mistakes. Most people have their own investment horror stories, such as opportunities missed, and I've got a good one. Even though I long ago "learned" the principles just recounted to you, apparently they didn't really register with me until I got kicked by the market a few times, such as happened on Friday, August 13, 1982.

I was planning to put some money into the stock market on that day by buying a small, but diversified, portfolio. Oh, I had timed the market "bottom," all right. The market had closed the previous day at 777 (on the Dow-Jones Industrial Average), a long-term low, and I felt a bull market looming because of Reaganomics. What more of a "buy signal" does an investor need?—777 on Friday the 13th! As I was reaching for the phone to call the broker, it rang. It was my old friend "Load Man" (another high school and college buddy, so nicknamed because of his dimensions, about 5'11", 310 lbs.), calling to set up a game of golf—for within the hour. O.K., let's play and I'll get into the market Monday. But the Dow went up 38 points while I was on the golf course and I decided to wait until some of that gain was given back, so I could get in nearer the bottom. I'm still waiting.

A year or two later, after telling this war story to another long-time friend (Load Man's brother, in fact, a bond trader from New Jersey, who himself was about 5'11", 275), we made a bet. I bet him $100 that the market would never see 777, or even 800, again. We set a reasonable time limit, four or five years hence, I believe, and I won. As sportsmen, we decided to play the debt off with a round of golf, double or nothing. Neither one of us played well that day— too much financial pressure, apparently—but I won by a stroke and received a check for $200 at the 19th hole. I am very pleased to have cashed in, at least in one small way, on my accurate market forecast after all, even though I realize intellectually that trying to predict the stock market is a futile exercise.

A glance at the holdings listed in the various parts of Table 2-7 may suggest that this section on the stock market is a case of "do as I say, not as I do." With understanding of the principles we have just reviewed, why have I not had a higher proportion of my assets in equities? ("Equities" is the high-finance term for stocks.) Most of my money has been in mutual funds that invest in bonds or money market instruments, not stocks. Why?

There are several reasons for this inconsistency, some of them even legitimate. First, recall that the guiding rule for maximizing your return from stock investing calls for always allocating as much of your money to stocks as possible, as much as you are comfortable with, as high a proportion of your assets as you can stand to put in stocks. It just happens that I have a very low risk tolerance. I am conservative. While in the process of building my initial nest egg, I have not been willing to accept the fluctuation and volatility of the stock market. Now that I have some wealth, a larger proportion of assets will be allocated to stocks, as that proportion has already been growing. Note, however, that the equities held, including the equity segment of my pension fund (CREF), are held indefinitely, thus far. The only exceptions have been one stock that was tendered in a buyout, and a small ownership interest in a local bar (which doesn't count for much because it was not serious money; it was considered sporting consumption).

Why do I violate the diversification principle by maintaining a concentration in one sector of the market, regional banks? I hold those for sentimental reasons irrelevant to our discussion. This anomaly does suggest another important principle, though. It has been proven that you cannot outperform the market, yet there is one sure-fire way of *exceeding* the market return! What? How can that be? Those two statements are directly contradictory. The answer is, it is not possible to beat the market's (buy-and-hold) return on a *risk-adjusted* basis, or at the same level of risk, that is. By incurring more risk (i.e., more variability or fluctuation in returns over time) you *can* earn a higher return—but it would be no higher on what is called a risk-adjusted basis; it would be no higher relative to the risk level assumed. If your time horizon is long enough, e.g., ten years or more, this strategy can be reasonable. Higher risk (volatility)-higher return portfolios would include international stocks and portfolios concentrated in one sector of the economy, such as I have done as shown in Tables 2-7(q-y). Yet the investor would still *buy and hold* within that portfolio to maximize return.

Another reason for my apparently irrational under-allocation to stocks is that I was not aware of how long my true time horizon was. For most of the period of Tables 2-7(d-n), I expected that I would need cash for a home purchase at any time. It just took me 13 years to make my purchase decision, not wanting to rush into anything. (The real estate agent did tell me that my sale was the most memorable and entertaining deal she had ever had.)

I can also plead ignorance. I didn't always know the investment principles I've explained here. Had I known or really internalized the information earlier, the allocation to equities throughout Table 2-7 probably would have been somewhat higher, despite the low visceral risk tolerance. At least we can't accuse the bottom lines in that table of being artificially inflated by abnormal stock market gains. Those numbers result from saving, pure and simple. So "do as I say" after all, up to your maximum stock market risk tolerance. If you still aren't convinced, if you need more evidence, check the references I've provided (footnote #7). Nobel Prize-winning economists will tell you the same thing I just did.

What about investment clubs? Investment clubs are like mini-mutual funds, groups of up to 25 people, who pool their money (typically through monthly dues) to invest in securities such as stocks. As you may be aware, these clubs tend to do pretty well. In fact, investment clubs, on average, do better than most professional money managers and mutual funds! The reason is that investment clubs generally follow a buy-and-hold philosophy, or very close to it, so they earn returns very close to the market average, which far surpasses most "professionals" and institutions.

Because of what you've just learned, armed with the information about investing principles you've received here, an investment club would probably be superfluous for you, and possibly frustrating. Truly, everything you need to know about stock market investing, to enable you to maximize your return, can be learned in under five seconds: "Buy and hold a diversified portfolio." Those five or six words are enough to transmit the return-maximizing rule. You are not going to learn anything of any value from sitting around a table in a club because you already know how to *maximize* your investment return, and nobody can teach you to do better than that. Might you get some good stock tips from investment club participation? Since it is not possible to outperform a stock-picking approach of throwing darts blindfolded, what good can stock tips do? Or suppose you join an investment club and find that you are the *only one* who understands the secret of maximizing performance, the only one familiar with the buy-and-hold principle. How would you like your chances of persuading others of that truth? Most laymen cannot believe the simple reality embodied in buy-and-hold because they cannot bring themselves to believe it. Perhaps it seems *too* simple. Many people seem to resist the principle because it is akin to being informed that there is no Santa Claus, as one of my colleagues puts it.

I found myself in that position once, and I do not wish it on you. I am the last who would ever join an investment club voluntarily, knowing what I know, but I allowed myself to be shanghaied into one once as a favor to the club's leader, an old friend. (I even served as President for awhile.) It was almost too funny. Before the end of my first meeting, it became obvious why this club had never made a dime, as it would have been to anyone with any real investment training. Not only had they lagged behind the market average, the group literally had made *no money* in its 20 years of operation—as I was able to deduce from simple estimation from available records. Almost every investment club in the world may do O.K., because doing so is a no-brainer, but this was the club "that couldn't shoot straight."

Their problem was self-"churning," or excessive turnover of their portfolio. They were constantly trading, buying and selling at every meeting, because it seemed to give them a sense that they were accomplishing something. As a result, this poor club was getting buried under transaction costs such as commissions. These costs literally wiped out any chance for profit, and the members didn't even realize what was happening. Not only were they all totally ignorant of the most rudimentary principles of investment, but they were not capable of the simple arithmetic needed to assess their own performance or even understand their own situation. This group was more interested in pretending to be sophisticated investors. To each his own.

These reflections suggest a basic guideline subscribed to by those who *are* in the investment club world: Affiliate with those who are like-minded, who have compatible perspectives. There were a handful of legitimate people in the group I fell in with, but most were small-time local businessmen posturing as big-timers, what are sometimes called "four-flushers" or phonies. That latter severe term applies by definition because the group's principal activity was talking about matters they knew nothing about. You know the type: They were morons when you knew them as kids or in high school, then they grow up and get a few bucks and think they're smart, but they haven't changed because they can't. (Witnessing that rare and pathetic combination of arrogance and ignorance can be amusing, but not necessarily if you have to be in the middle of it.)

Now suppose there is an investment club with one member who knows the most important basic principles of stock investing, while all the rest do not and never will because they are not equipped to. Would that violate the "like-minded" and "compatible" criteria? Is that the position you might find yourself in were you to club up, given what you now know? Though most clubs seem to approach buy-and-hold results, good luck finding a club that really understands market efficiency. The general public does not seem to be up to it, by and large. Do yourself a favor and avoid investment clubs. You don't need them and, frankly, you are now beyond them.

There's No Place Like Home

Purchasing a home probably should be considered more of a consumption decision than an investment decision. Of prime importance is obtaining a dwelling with the operational characteristics you and your family need, e.g., size, number of rooms of various kinds desired, garage, location, comfort, aesthetics, etc. This is not exactly news to you. Yet there also is an obvious capital investment aspect to purchasing a residence because it is a fixed asset whose value can grow over time, sometimes substantially. Of course, home purchase is generally the largest single expenditure an individual or family ever makes.

Now, I am not exactly Mr. Real Estate. You may have far more experience than I have in the residential real estate market. You can't have much less because I have only purchased one unit, a condominium. Yet that one purchase was extraordinarily successful in large part because of certain underlying principles—some basic principles about which there seems to be some public confusion. When making a home purchase decision, it is important to keep the following things in mind.

I. First, you have probably heard all about the benefits of the mortgage interest deduction. Home mortgage interest payments are tax-deductible. Do not, however, make the mistake of exaggerating the value of this benefit, as some overzealous salespeople in the real estate and mortgage lending industries encourage. The mortgage interest deduction is not _savings_ per se. It does not _earn_ you any money, it only _reduces_ your income tax liability. This tax benefit only means that your net cost or outflow is a little less than it would otherwise be without deductibility. It is a discount—no more, no less. If you have a $2000 mortgage interest federal tax _deduction_, and are in the 31% tax bracket, this just means that your net interest cost is reduced by $620.

179

But wouldn't you rather not have a mortgage, if you could afford to pay cash for a home, and reduce your net interest cost to zero?

The point is that the deductibility of mortgage interest is a benefit the government gives you if you *have* to pay mortgage interest. It is only a true benefit if you have to have a mortgage and pay that interest anyway. The benefit is limited to your marginal tax rate (bracket) *times* the amount of your deduction. By no means should you incur more mortgage debt, and the accompanying payments, than you have to.

But what about building *equity* through your monthly mortgage payment? Put more down up front and you've already got that equity. A mortgage and its interest are a high price to pay for the privilege of building equity more slowly. Again, this is only a good deal if you have to get a mortgage to be able to buy a home. Do as this book instructs, and you may be in a position to buy a home for cash. Otherwise, from a financial perspective, the rule is to put as much money down as possible to minimize your debt and interest owed. (Getting a 15-year, instead of 30-year, mortgage helps build equity faster and reduces interest costs, though involves higher payments.) The only exception, as mentioned before, is if you are *sure* the return you can earn on your money is greater than the mortgage interest rate after taxes.

For instance, if the historical return on common stocks is 10-12%, and you can obtain a mortgage for 7-8%, why not borrow? Say the expected before-tax return on invested funds is 11% with a cost of borrowed funds (the mortgage rate) of 7.5%—which would be 7.9% and 5.4%, respectively, after taxes for someone in the 28% bracket. That is an attractive spread but, remember, it is an *expectation* of 7.9% versus a *known* cost of 5.4%. Since the stock market has performed so well in recent decades, until very recently, perhaps we are in for a prolonged cycle of returns below the long-term norm. The decision really depends on your risk preference and risk aversion.

However, if you can invest in a tax-deferred instrument, such as a tax-deferred annuity or an SRA (supplemental retirement account) available through your employer, the case for borrowing becomes stronger.

Then it is a comparison of *11%* expected return (less the net present value of taxes deferred into the distant future) and a 5.4% after-tax cost of funds. Yet tax-deferred annuities are available from investment companies only at substantial management fees, which may lop off a couple of percentage points from your expected return. With an SRA, you may be capable of investing only a small fraction of the amount of funds borrowed. Again, an uncertain gain measured against a certain cost is for those with a risk preference.

II. What about appreciation of the real estate's value? That happens anyway whether you have a mortgage or own the property outright, so it is not a factor. But this leads us to the next general guideline: Make sure you identify *all relevant costs*, as well as benefits, when evaluating alternative homes for purchase or when deciding whether to rent or buy.

Some of these costs are obvious. For instance, is any difference in charges for utilities foreseeable with House A vs. House B vs. your present apartment? What about expected annual maintenance cost for a house, which would not apply to the apartment? Likewise, real estate taxes, mortgage interest, and insurance have to be considered. Not to be forgotten, emphatically, are two less visible costs. Any appreciation in real estate value of an owned home is a *cost* of the alternative of renting, along with actual rent paid. Then there is the *opportunity cost* of any down payment for a home purchase. Whatever you would have been able to earn on that money is a hidden cost of home ownership. To illustrate, the worksheet comparing relevant costs for my own apartment vs. condominium purchase decision appears as Table 8-3.

With such a close call financially between two choices (and a third in my case, a different condo), it becomes time to look at secondary factors. I considered such things as (1) one-car vs. two-car garage; (2) traffic in the neighborhood; (3) where's the nearest supermarket (God love 'em); (4) what about the flood plain? (5) Is the mail box attached or do I have to walk outside to retrieve the damn mail? and (6) proximity to my most common destinations. I literally projected to the penny (and minute) my expected annual difference in travel cost to the coun-

TABLE 8-3

Actual "Own vs. Rent" Monthly Cost Comparison
(Spring 1993)

Rental Expense		Ownership Expense	
Rent	$445	Condo Fee	$147
Utilities	84	Real estate taxes (net)	56
Appreciation[a]	250	Utilities	150
	$779	Interior maintenance	10
		Opportunity cost[b]	420
			$783

[a]Estimated on the basis of 20-year historical trend of condo prices.
[b]Estimated from long-term average after-tax stock market return.

try club, my favorite bars, my parents' home, and my office (not in order of priority), with regard to my three choices.

Attend to details such as these, and you should be able to make a good home purchase. You can also find self-help books in the library to guide you through the process. Also seek the advice of a realtor (pronounced reel'-ter, not re'-la-ter) you can trust.

Sorry, I can't tell you a thing about how to buy a car.

Remember, It's Only a Game

Well, no, it's not *only* a game. Getting rich without making very much money is not merely a game, but there is a *competitive challenge* dimension to it that can provide entertainment. There is an element of doing the seemingly impossible, or knowing what others don't know and profiting from that knowledge, that can be stimulating and satisfying. To enable you to fully enjoy the *sporting* aspect of getting rich without making very much money, the Professor has some final advice for you that may be superfluous. If so, all the better.

It is inconceivable that you could derive full enjoyment from a game if you were to not play by the rules. Cheating, or doing anything unfair or unethical, would spoil the fun for almost anyone. Therefore, I suggest you not even consider cheating on taxes. Not only would such behavior undermine the fun of the wholesome endeavor described in this book, but the risk-to-reward ratio makes it imprudent. It is not even necessary, as the honestly-achieved numbers of Chapter 2's tables reveal. (Would I publicly report them, along with such abnormal saving rates, if they were not?) Sure, the government allows and expects you to take every available and legitimate tax deduction, but nothing beyond that is needed. Realistically, in *our* tax brackets rates are low enough anyway. (This is not to be inferred as endorsement of the present structure of federal income taxes. Even lower rates would undoubtedly be better for the country, including the federal treasury.) Since you and I don't make very much money to begin with, the disparity in relative outcomes between honor and dishonor in this regard is not great enough to make a meaningful difference. No matter how much you have come to appreciate small amounts of money, as you should have by now, no one needs to obtain them that way.

Chapter 9

Recapitulation, Reinforcement, and Extension of Principles: Putting it All Together

It is hard to believe that more people haven't figured all this out. Getting rich without making much money is not only relatively easy, it should be almost inevitable if you set the process in motion the right way—if you lay the proper groundwork. Fortunately, that part of it doesn't require much on your part. Here's the program:

1. The beginning of step #1 is to realize that it really is possible to become wealthy without making very much money. Case examples provided in Chapter 2 are sufficient to demonstrate that opportunity, but you don't need to trust me. Mrs. Amy Dacyczyn, editor of *The Tightwad Gazette* cited for you earlier, and her husband saved over $87,000 including capital investment in a seven-year period, *in addition to* a down payment on a $125,000 home on a seven-acre tract. This was done on the husband's salary which was never more than *$30,000* during that time span.[1] (You might not consider their kind of money *rich*, but the Dacyczyns have four children!) A 38-year-old Texas man, Jim Steamer, and his wife accumulated $230,000 in ten years even though their combined income averaged *less than $20,000*.[2] Chapter 2 details a saving performance record of half a million dollars in eight years (which may indeed be a "record" relative to the low income).

How can *low income* translate into *great wealth*? That false paradox is resolved by understanding the difference between the two variables. Income is a flow over time, wealth is a quantity at a point in time. Income and wealth apply to different contexts, and are appraised on different scales. Little money earned can be equivalent to a large amount of wealth if even a moderate share of the income is retained over time. That retention, surplus, or "personal profit," is the key. If you can just hang onto a reasonable fraction of the dollars that flow through your possession, you, or anyone, can become rich. Or even "If we'd saved all the money we ever wasted, all of us would be millionaires," as says the renowned financial writer Jane Bryant Quinn.[3] Very true, but how? How does one save, after never having been able to? All you need is the right attitude.

2. Knowledge of the realities of point #1 above should go a long way toward establishing the frame of mind that enables the possibility of easy wealth to be actualized. Once you know that the kind of wealth gain shown in the Chapter 1 and 2 tables is really possible for you, you should be favorably inclined toward doing whatever it takes to make it happen, especially when you realize how little it does take. It really doesn't require any action on your part *at all*. It is instead a matter of what you *don't* do.

Isn't that a pleasant situation for you to be in—to be able to get rich without making very much money, and without even having to do anything? What could be better? What could be easier? Wouldn't it be *fun* to have a few hundred thousand dollars a few years from now, as has been proven possible even *at or near minimum wage*? Wouldn't it be *enjoyable* to accomplish something like that, to do what other people ignorantly think is not possible? Wouldn't it be *satisfying* to demonstrate that you are different from the rest, more clever than those who don't know what you now know? Are you feeling the stirrings of the right attitude coming on?

You want attitude? I'll give you attitude. Here's attitude:

A teacher in New York began investing in stocks. After a few years, he quit teaching and got a job with the fire department. Why? The extra free time firemen have gave him more time to track his investments. By his late 50's he had accumulated a net worth of more than *$5 million*. He continued with his department, living on his fireman's salary until retirement, because he didn't want to lose his pension![4]

Do you think that attitude arose only *after* that man became rich, or was it there before? Do you suppose the attitude might have been what led to that teacher/fireman becoming rich? (And I'll bet he used the buy-and-hold strategy for his investing.)

3. You do not have to *do* anything to get rich without making very much money unless you consider a *decision* to be an action. You do have to decide to *let* it all happen. Is that too much for you? Once you make that decision, which should follow naturally from your newly found understanding and attitude, that is *almost* all there is to it. That alone should prompt you in the right direction. If you need more help than that, don't worry; it is available. Plenty of help is available. If, after all this, you still don't have the internal *inclination* that inevitably will make you rich easily, just play some tricks—on yourself. Those tricks are outlined in Chapter 3. If you need to *manipulate* your psyche into cooperating, into allowing and facilitating your rapid wealth gain, be sure to employ those psychological devices described in Chapter 3 that were proven effective long before I gave them to you. (I was struck by a poignant irony after spending many hours, over several weeks, word-processing this manuscript into my old Mac personal computer. After clicking on the "save" command probably a thousand times or more, I finally realized the connection to the subject matter. Save. Save. Save. Save. Maybe we should add one more psychological manipulation to your bag of tricks. If you are finding it difficult to save money, just do copious amounts of word processing on the Mac or PC, and the right message should be implanted subliminally.)

4. *Of course* saving money is part of the regimen for getting rich without making very much money. You can't save money? By now you know why that is a ludicrous assertion. So many people who don't even make *squat* have amassed such fantastic saving records, that it is time for you to stop objecting. Stop making excuses and start emulating the achievers. Financial expert J. B. Quinn documents that "people can save on earnings as low as $10,000 a year."[5] Again, if I can save on a salary of $4000 (about $9000 in 2008 dollars) . . . !

Do you need more incentive to save? Just remember, a penny saved is *not* a penny earned. With taxes, both federal and state income and Social Security, a penny saved amounts to about *two* pennies earned. It takes close to two pennies earned for a penny to drop to the bottom line.[6] Save that penny in the first place, and it's already there on the bottom line.

Can't save? Don't forget the phenomenal saving rates shown in Chapter 2 and elsewhere. Again, you don't need to believe me. Personal finance expert Humberto Cruz of the *Chicago Tribune* reports an *after-tax* saving rate of 66% for himself and his wife. Then there's that guy in Texas—$200,000 in ten years on minimum wage![7]

O.K., forget the big picture and focus on the little picture. A series of our little pictures adds up to the big picture you want. Don't ever neglect or under-appreciate the *small* amounts of money. ("Treat them well and they'll treat you well.") They add up to large amounts of money and, through compounding, multiply into *very* large amounts of money. As one prominent financial expert expressed it on this very point in *The Wall Street Journal*: "Everyone looks for this one great idea that will help them save more. Doing one thing differently never makes much of a difference. It is all the little things that you do that really matter."[8]

Here's a hint, a clue: Power is great to have, isn't it? Whether you have ever had any power, or can only imagine what it is like to have power, you surely can know what the possession of power signifies: the ability to impose your will upon others, the ability to direct things in accordance with your will, being able to have things the way you want them to be.

Does that sound like fun—to be able to make sure that the things in your life are the way you want? Isn't that what life is all about?

One thing most people do not understand about power is that it is more valuable to you if it is *not* exercised. Exercising or applying power *uses it up*, and leaves you with less. It is best if you use your power judiciously, sparingly, to conserve and retain it as much as possible. Money is power, to a large extent. There is considerable operational overlap between money and power. Once you start to retain (save) some money, that gives you some power—if only buying power at the beginning, more power over time. Don't throw that power away needlessly. Don't spend your money (power) unless it is on a very worthy purpose. Learning this will help you appreciate that *not spending your money* is more fun and valuable and productive to you than spending your money! Think of the long-term consequences of the two alternatives, and that should reinforce the right attitude and behavior.

Power does not mean action; it means the *potential* to act. That potential is freedom, by definition. Do you need to be reminded of the value of such an ability or potential? Mrs. Dacyczyn of *The Tightwad Gazette* reveals her understanding when she says, "Just because we are free to consume doesn't mean we have to,"[9] and "If you're frugal, you have plenty of money in the bank. I could pull a lever right now and take a trip to Hawaii if I wanted to. But I don't want to."[10] Is that not a nice position to be in—to be able to pull the lever but elect *not* to? That is real power. Isn't that cool? Have that attitude, and you will get rich.

Of course, with more money comes greater power, more than you ever imagined you could have. So go ahead and throw that power away, by throwing your money away. See if I care. That just leaves more of both for the rest of us. I'll take the philosopher Henry David Thoreau over that idiocy. As Thoreau said, "A man is rich in proportion to the number of things which he can afford to let alone."[11] So doing, in turn, makes you richer and more powerful. From that standing comes the potential or the power to have anything you want in the future. All it takes is a little temperance, a little forbearance, in the present and you can have broad freedom in the future—the *near* future.

Once again, no action is necessary to get rich without making very much money, just a decision, a *choice*. You don't have to *stop* spending to get rich, just limit your spending to the things that are really important to you. Being able to identify those things is a key element of our program. You can still spend plenty of money and not compromise your preferred lifestyle, as I have proven. You just have to choose *less* than the full range of alternatives. Is that not reasonable? Tactically, start with a target of zero for every spending category, and work back from there.

5. Naturally, exhortations to save money and get rich would not be legitimate unless the *means* of doing so were also provided. The most crucial of those means have just been reviewed—having the right attitude, which sets everything else in motion. Ingredients of that attitude, knowledge and understanding, are now yours for the taking as well. Motivations to inculcate the attitude are also at hand, as abundantly and presently reiterated.

In addition, for any prospective money savers and rich-getters who need a boost, or need some creativity, in doing those little things that add up to big money, there are Chapters 5 and 6 on saving tactics. Don't be put off by some of the more extreme entries, my personal disclosures included. Those examples are offered as a laundry list of devices for you to choose from. Select any reasonable subset and you will be well on your way. If you already do *all* those things listed, you're already rich— no matter how little you earn—and don't need any help from anybody!

Here's a test. If you are the type who uses up pencils down to the stub, to the point of getting lead on the fingers, or if you squeeze every last dollop out of the toothpaste tube before discarding, you *will* get rich. If you use things up to that degree, as someone I know does, you will get rich because either (a) you are able to force or discipline yourself into doing it, indicating that you will be capable of the same middling self-control in other areas which, in turn, leads to wealth; or (b) you do this *naturally*, which means you already have the proper wealth-generating attitude, with the desired bottom-line results following automatically. (As revealed in Chapter 3, self-discipline—*a*, above—is not *necessary* for our wealth-gain program to succeed. It is but one possible approach.)

6. Then, as long as you're going to be saving and accumulating money, you might as well learn how to put those dollars to work for you the best, most advantageous, way possible. You have been exposed to some rare information on investing, actually the ultimate answer on the subject, that is understood by only a select few. (Your stockbroker understands it, but s/he is not about to tell you.) Once this information finds its way to the general public, it will be a major scandal; i.e., blindfolded chimpanzees throwing darts, on average, outperform the universe of investment professionals. In the meantime, you can use this information to your own benefit, to maximize the return on your investment dollars. The section of Chapter 8 on investment may also yield some valuable examples of what *not* to do, frankly, while Chapter 7 has some guidance for prospective entrepreneurs.

So our step-by-step procedure can now be summarized as a simple sequence of (1) *awareness* and *understanding* of the possibility of actually getting rich without making a lot of money, which leads to (2) the properly favorable *attitude* toward such an eventuality. From there, things should fall into place. (3) All you need is a free and natural choice, or *decision*, to go in that direction, to allow it to happen for you. (Why not? What have you got to lose?) (4) This decision prompts the correct *action* or behavior patterns—except it is more accurately described as *in*action. It is all a matter of what you *don't* do. (5) For your assistance and success, supplementary *means* are also provided, to help you adhere to the correct path of saving and enrichment, to reinforce your direction, if you even need such aid at that point. (6) Then, we might as well *follow-up* by maximizing the probability that you will be managing your new wealth as rationally as possible. Every dollar *grown* as well as saved goes straight to the bottom line, too, and then generates even more dollars for you. A simple program, indeed. More people should have been able to figure this out.

Economics is known as a dismal and dreary science, but at the individual level it needn't be. I hope the message of how much fun this endeavor can be has been received—how rewarding and even amusing it is to get rich, without having to make very much money. It can be great sport.

Lest anyone come away with the wrong impression, one other point needs to be clarified. This book has been about personal pecuniary enrichment, one particular and universally accessible approach to personal wealth. This theme, however, does not imply that that is all there is to life. Some other books are about baseball. Some books are about religion. Some books are about chemistry. The topic of this book is not tantamount to advocacy that getting rich is the only thing in life any more than one would conclude that the only thing in life is baseball or chemistry. Each of those domains has a role in the full montage of life. Of course, ensuring your financial well-being, especially if you didn't know how to do it previously, has a major role to play in life, and is well-deserving of at least the brief attention you and I have given it here.

Continuing on this modest issue of what life is all about, and identifying what is most important to you, let me leave you with some philosophy I share with my students at the end of each semester. If you haven't yet established some fundamental life objectives for yourself, i.e., decided what you really want to do with your life, it is time you thought about it. In that regard, I have two suggestions that may seem unorthodox, initially. First, try defining your objectives in terms of *process* rather than *outcome*. What does that mean? The problem with an objective expressed as an outcome, a result, or an end-state, is that you always face the dilemma of either (a) not having achieved the objective or (b) no longer having the objective to strive for (once it has been met). Process-based objectives, on the other hand, are amenable to ongoing fulfillment in the present, not just one-time-only accomplishment in the future or past as is the case with an objective stated as an outcome.

For example, there is a university professor I know very well whose paramount career objective is to make the *maximum possible contribution* to the welfare of his school. Sure, there is a way of expressing that aim in terms of result, such as to become Notre Dame's greatest scholar, teacher, or benefactor. But expression of the objective in terms of the process itself allows current and continuing fulfillment, rather than *only* deferred, future accomplishment. As long as this professor is *doing* everything he can for his school (the process), the objective is fully satisfied. It is as the great basketball coach, John Wooden, defined success: "Success is peace of mind from knowing that you are doing your very best to be the best you can possibly become." Again, the emphasis is on the process. So long as you are *doing* your best, success and fulfillment are achieved, regardless of the ultimate outcome. Keep this in mind, and give it a try.

Related suggestion number two: Try to devote yourself and your life to higher purposes than *just* your own enrichment or aggrandizement. Not that gaining material wealth is not a worthy aim, as we have explained in these pages, but try to find a more elevated overriding purpose for your life if you can. That objective might be something like becoming a good, productive functionary of capitalism, the economic system that has delivered more prosperity and liberty to more people than any other system ever invented. Or it could be something as straightforward as providing for your family's welfare. Conventionally altruistic pursuits such as contributing to charity may also fit the bill. The point is that, if you do dedicate yourself fundamentally to the more lofty purposes, almost everything you do in life becomes more meaningful, more rewarding, more satisfying, and more *fun*, because it is more important. Of course, attending to the material things first, by getting rich, can be very helpful in advancing the higher purposes.

It can provide the resources that allow your altruism to be directed anywhere your conscience takes you. Try this also. As a famous person once said, "Do this in remembrance of me."

Where do I get off advising altruism and elevated purposes? Didn't I admit to self-interest in writing this book? Give me a break, please. Remember, there is a mix of motives on my part, appropriately. *Of course*, self-interest is part of it. Almost everyone works for money. Do you know of anyone who would work for nothing? I know of some, but not many people. In a free-market economy, however, the enlightened provider of goods or services understands that to get, one must give. If I want to make money (for a change), I must do something for others, whether providing manual labor or whatever. Without doubt, the very best product I can think of to offer readers is the ability to get rich without making very much money—a rare ability, unfortunately, that rightfully should become much more common. I'm doing my part. My ultimate aim here may have been normal self-interest, but the instrumental goal, i.e., the instrument by which the ultimate goal is achieved, has been your welfare. You're welcome.

One other objective should be a mutual motivator for us. Surely you have noticed the recurring concern about the low national saving rate. We need to do something about that, because of the manifold economic benefits a higher saving rate would produce for our country and our people (or any nation and people with a similar problem). Your adoption of the principles portrayed in this book would make a contribution, and if you are moved to join the team, others will be too. Collectively, we can have a real impact, and it just might beneficially affect the long-term trend of our economy. Now *there* is an "elevated and lofty" objective worthy of your consideration. And I did not claim I had *only* two motives, did I?

Even if you are now well-motivated, are you still skeptical about your chances to gain the kind of financial success we describe? Don't be, if you haven't even tried the program yet! What sense does that make? At least try those methods of Chapter 3 before you give it up. Is that too much to expect of yourself, given the high stakes? And then don't forget the fall-back strategy. If all else fails (and it probably won't), "just do it" or "just say no."

I'll tell you what: After reading this, the next time you are about to spend some money you don't need to spend, *just don't do it* and see what happens. Bank the money instead, as a kind of experiment. You never know what it might lead to (other than more money in your pocket). Who knows? Maybe you'll write a book.

Good luck, although you shouldn't need it any more.

Endnotes

CHAPTER 2

1. This illustration comes from the sydicated personal finance columnist, Humberto Cruz, in "Savings: How to save a million bucks," *Chicago Tribune*, June 23, 1995, "Your Money" section.
2. Humberto Cruz, "Savings: Getting there from here," *Chicago Tribune*, July 21, 1994, "Your Money" section.
3. Humberto Cruz, "Savings: No need to deprive yourself," *Chicago Tribune*, May 12, 1995, "Your Money" section.
4. Sam Beard, "Minimum-Wage Millionaires," *The Wall Street Journal*, Aug. 14, 1995.
5. Marilyn vos Savant, "Ask Marilyn," *Parade Magazine*, June 25, 1995, p. 8.

CHAPTER 3

1. "Asceticism," *Encyclopaedia Brittanica*, Vol. 2, (Chicago: Encyclopaedia Brittanica, Inc., 1961), p. 500.
2. *Ibid.*, pp. 500-501.
3. Carl E. Thoreson and Michael J. Mahoney, *Behavioral Self-Control* (New York: Holt, Rinehart and Winston, Inc., 1974); Brian T. Yates, *Self-Management: The Science and Art of Helping Yourself* (Belmont, CA: Wadsworth Publishing Company, 1985).
4. Thoreson and Mahoney, *op. cit.*, p. 30.
5. Yates, *op. cit.*, p. 110.
6. Thoreson and Mahoney, *op. cit.*, p. 119.
7. Yates, *op. cit.*, p. 121.
8. Adapted from Thoreson and Mahoney, *op. cit.*, p. 120.
9. Thoreson and Mahoney, *op. cit.*, p. 73.
10. Yates, *op. cit.*, p. 47.
11. *Ibid.*, p. 38.
12. Thoreson and Mahoney, *op. cit.*, p. 41.
13. *Ibid.*, p. 63.
14. *Ibid.*, p. 7.

CHAPTER 4

1. Bernard Wysocki, Jr., "Binge Buyers: Many Baby Boomers Save Little, May Run Into Trouble Later On," *The Wall Street Journal*, June 5, 1995, p. 1.
2. Thomas T. Vogel, Jr., "Americans, Notoriously Poor Savers, Are Doing Better," *The Wall Street Journal*, Feb. 9, 1996.
3. *Ibid.*
4. B. Wysocki, *op. cit.*, p. A5.
5. Clint Willis, "Retirement Planning: The Personality Factor," *Fidelity Focus*, Spring 1995, pp. 5-8.
6. *Ibid.*
7. Amy Wilson, "A Penny Saved," *The Post-Tribune*, June 6, 1992, pp. D3-D4, quoting author Linda Bowman.
8. Richard C. Young, "The 36 Greatest Joys of Wealth," *Financial Intelligence*, May 1992, pp. 6-7.
9. C. Willis, *op. cit.*, pp. 7-8.
10. David Foster, "A generation discovering that less is more," *Naples (FL) Daily News*, Feb. 7, 1993, p. 14A.
11. Mary Iorio, "Yuppies: Down and out in the '90s," *USA Weekend*, April 2-4, 1993, p. 28.
12. Thomas J. Stanley, "How to Live Like a Millionaire," *Reader's Digest*, January 1993, pp. 58-59; condensed from *Medical Economics*, July 20, 1992.
13. *Ibid.*, pp. 57, 59.
14. "Rich and Infamous," *Investment Vision*, Aug.-Sept. 1991, p. 13.
15. John Rothchild, "Skinflint Chic," *Investment Vision*, July-August 1990, pp. 12-13.
16. T. Stanley, *op. cit.*, pp. 58-59.

CHAPTER 5

1. Vanessa O'Connell, "Yes, You Really Can Boost Your Savings in 1996," *The Wall Street Journal*, Dec. 29, 1995, p. C1.
2. "Cost of raising babies seen doubling in U.S.," *South Bend Tribune*, Dec. 17, 1989.
3. Humberto Cruz, "Obstacle course: Report lists the 6 main barriers to saving enough for retirement," *Chicago Tribune*, May 5, 1995.
4. Paul W. McCracken, "Why Deficits Matter," *The Wall Street Journal*, Dec. 26, 1995.

5. Humberto Cruz, "Second Opinion: Readers sound off on why people find it difficult to save," *Chicago Tribune*, May 19, 1995. Jonathan Clements, "When Retirement Experts Talk, Why Doesn't Anybody Listen?" *The Wall Street Journal*, June 20, 2007, p. D1. "Can Your Retirement Nest Egg Really Grow Too Large?" in *In the Vanguard* (Valley Forge, PA: The Vanguard Group, Inc., 2007), Summer, p. 16.

6. Guy E. Churchill, *Compound Interest Simplified* (Oxford, England: Pergamon Press, 1969), pp. 6-7.

7. Adapted from *ibid.*, pp. 5-6.

8. *Basic Statistics: Price Indexes* (New York: Standard & Poor, 1994), p. 76; U.S. Dept. of Commerce, Bureau of Economic Analysis, *Business Statistics 1963-91* (Washington, DC: U.S. Government Printing Office, June 1992).

CHAPTER 6

1. As reported in *Family Circle*, April 4, 1995, p. 53.

2. Frank James, "When money's no object of desire," *Chicago Tribune*, Jan. 12, 1992, Sec. 5, pp. 1, 4; Brad Lemley, "How To Save A Buck," *Parade Magazine*, Mar. 17, 1991, pp. 4-6; M. Iorio, *op. cit.*

3. From Glenn Burkins, "Personal Finance: Fine line between frugal, cheap," *Chicago Tribune*, Apr. 14, 1993; Humberto Cruz, "Top 40 principles of savings," *Chicago Tribune*, Apr. 15, 1993; Liz Pulliam, "Managing your finances can yield big rewards," *Chicago Tribune*, Sept. 13, 1994, Sec. 6, p. 3; Robert Heady, "Game plan: Making the right financial moves now could mean survival in '96," *Chicago Tribune*, Jan. 3, 1996.

4. Jane Bryant Quinn, "Money Facts: 20 Surefire Ways to Save," *Woman's Day*, June 28, 1994, p. 28.

5. Rebecca E. Greer, "Money: 170 Ways to Pinch Pennies—Painlessly," *Woman's Day*, July 21, 1992, pp. 44-52; Franny Van Nevel, "102 Ways Not to Spend Money," *Woman's Day*, Jan. 10, 1995, pp. 59-63.

6. R. E. Greer, *op. cit.*, p. 46.

7. G. Burkins, *op. cit.*

CHAPTER 7

1. Before any reader trained in statistics jumps on this, I did say *about* five-to-one. You do have to adjust for some joint conditions like homers in more than one of the three games, or multiple homers per game, but the 5-1 estimate in the text is close enough.

2. Andrew Tobias, "How To Invest--The Smart Way," *Parade Magazine*, Jan. 21, 1996, p. 14.

3. Again, in deference to probability precision, these are approximations. Technically, the miniscule joint probability of winning more than one sweepstakes would have to be deducted from the cumulative probability, or added to the odds.

4. Tom Ainslie, *The Compleat Horseplayer* (New York: Pocket Books, 1969).

5. *Ibid.*, p. xx.

CHAPTER 8

1. A. Tobias, *op. cit.*, p. 15.

2. Table developed with assistance of information from undated literature published by Kemper Investments, "Have you forgotten about your IRA?" (#MKTCOM-21).

3. Derived from undated literature published by United Services Funds, "Starting early really *pays*!" (#SSF600).

4. Adapted from Roger G. Ibbotson and Rex A. Sinquefield, *Stocks, Bonds, Bills and Inflation (SBBI), 1982*, updated in *Stocks, Bonds, Bills and Inflation 1990 Yearbook* (Chicago: Ibbotson Associates Inc.).

5. "Vanguard's Investment Philosophy: 'We Believe' #9," *Vanguard Investment Counseling & Research* (Valley Forge, PA: The Vanguard Group, Inc., 2006). *Stocks, Bonds, Bills and Inflation 1996 Yearbook*[TM], (Chicago: Ibbotson Associates).

6. "Back to Basics: The ABCs of Investing," *Insights* (a publication of T. Rowe Price Associates), Vol. 1, No. 216.

7. For further explanation and substantiation see: Eugene F. Fama, "Efficient Capital Markets: A Review of Theory and Empirical Work," *The Journal of Finance*, May 1970, pp. 383-417; Paul A. Samuelson, "Challenge to Judgment," *The Journal of Portfolio Man-*

agement, Vol. 1, No. 1, Fall 1974, pp. 17-19; Paul A. Samuelson, "The Judgment of Economic Science on Rational Portfolio Management: Indexing, Timing, and Long-Horizon Effects," *The Journal of Portfolio Management,* Fall 1989, pp. 4-12; Burton G. Malkiel, *A Random Walk Down Wall Street,* 4th Ed. (New York: Morton, 1985); Charles C. Mann, "Fama's Market," *Investment Vision,* Oct./Nov. 1991, pp. 52-55; Eugene F. Fama, "Efficient Capital Markets: II," *The Journal of Finance,* Dec. 1991, pp. 1575-1617.

CHAPTER 9

1. B. Lemley, *op. cit.,* p. 4.
2. Jonathan Clements, "A Miserly Grip on the Purse Strings Can Help Boost Retirement Savings," *The Wall Street Journal,* Dec. 12, 1995, p. C1.
3. J. B. Quinn, *op. cit.*
4. T. J. Stanley, *op. cit.,* p. 58.
5. J. B. Quinn, *op. cit.*
6. A. Tobias, *op. cit.,* p. 14.
7. Humberto Cruz, "Savings: Not your average Joes," *Chicago Tribune,* Sept. 9, 1993; J. Clements, *op. cit.*
8. V. O'Connell, *op. cit.*
9. A. Wilson, *op. cit.,* p. D4.
10. F. James, *op. cit.,* Sec. 5, p. 4.
11. Henry David Thoreau, *Walden* (Boston: The Riverside Press Cambridge, 1957), p. 56.

About the Author

John F. Gaski is Associate Professor of Marketing at the University of Notre Dame. His degrees include a BBA and MBA from Notre Dame, and an M.S. and Ph.D. from the University of Wisconsin at Madison. He is the author of over 90 published articles, papers, and monographs which have appeared in the *Journal of Marketing, Journal of Marketing Research, Journal of Consumer Research, Journal of the Academy of Marketing Science, Journal of Business Ethics, Journal of Public Policy & Marketing, Journal of Consumer Policy, Review of Marketing, Research in Marketing, European Journal of Marketing, Industrial Marketing Management, International Journal of Physical Distribution & Logistics Management, Advances in Distribution Channel Research, Advances in Financial Economics, Business Horizons, Psychology & Marketing, International Journal of Management, The Journal of European Economic History, Business and Society Review, Social Behavior and Personality, Sociological Spectrum, Psychological Reports, Perceptual and Motor Skills,* the *Journal of Educational Psychology,* and the *International Journal on World Peace,* as well as proceedings of leading professional associations. Primary research interests are power in distribution channels and the societal impact of marketing activity. Courses taught include Marketing Management, Marketing Strategy and Planning, Marketing Research, and Distribution Management, at both the graduate and undergraduate levels.

Professor Gaski serves or has served on the editorial review boards of the *Journal of Marketing, Journal of the Academy of Marketing Science, Journal of Marketing Channels,* and *Journal of Education for Business,* is a member of the Beta Gamma Sigma, Mu Kappa Tau, and Alpha Mu Alpha honorary societies, and was selected one of the "100 Best Researchers in Marketing" by a peer review study (published in *Marketing Educator,* 1997). He has had his commentary published in the *Chicago Tribune, Chicago Sun-Times, Indianapolis Star, Investor's Business Daily, The Center Magazine, Human Events,* and *Contemporary Review,* and is recognized in various Who's Who lists.

John Gaski was born in Gary, Indiana in 1949, and then moved to the small nearby town of Crown Point when he was eight months old because he didn't like it in Gary, taking his parents with him.

CORBY BOOKS....Check Us Out....

Corby in a new, innovative publisher with a diverse and interesting line of books. For the dedicated Notre Dame clan, we offer *CELEBRATING NOTRE DAME*, a lavish coffee-table photographic view of the campus, by Matt Cashore, with text by Kerry Temple. A close look at life on campus is the subject of *KNOWN BY NAME: Inside The Halls of Notre Dame*, by Fr. James King, Rector of Sorin Hall. For the family, we have *CREATING HAPPY MEMORIES: 101 Ways to Start and Strengthen Family Traditions*, by Pam Ogren, and *ST. NICHOLAS IN AMERICA: Christmas as Holy Day and Holiday*, by Fr. Nicholas Ayo. Business executives will benefit from *BUSINESS WISE GUIDE: 80 Powerful Insights You Can't Learn in Business School*, by Mark O. Hubbard and *STOKE THE FIRE WITHIN: A Guide to Igniting Your Life* by motivational speaker Charlie Adams. Other new titles include *I HAD LUNCH WITH GOD: Biblical Inspirations for Tough Times* by Dr. Kathy Sullivan, *NONPROFIT GOVERNANCE: The Who What and How of Nonprofit Boardship* by Thomas Harvey and John Tropman, *MAY I HAVE YOUR ATTENTION PLEASE: Tales from the Notre Dame Pressbox*, by Mike Collins and Sgt. Tim McCarthy, *THE FORGOTTEN FOUR: Notre Dame's Greatest Backfield and the 1953 Undefeated Season*, by Donald Hubbard and Mark Hubbard, *THE GEESMAN GAME* by Wes Doi and Chris Geesman, and *THE HEART OF NOTRE DAME: Spiritual Reflections for Students, Parents, Alumni and Friends* by NicholasAyo, CSC

For full details, log on to corbypublishing.com